Irish
Broad Gauge Carriages

A Pictorial Introduction

Desmond Coakham

Irish Broad Gauge Carriages
Desmond Coakham © 2004

ISBN 1 85780 175 X

First published in 2004 by Midland Publishing
4 Watling Drive, Hinckley, Leics, LE10 3EY, England.
Tel: 01455 233747 Fax: 01455 233737
E-mail: midlandbooks@compuserve.com

Design concept and layout, © Midland Publishing and
Stephen Thompson Associates

Midland Publishing is an imprint of
Ian Allan Publishing Ltd.

Printed in England by Ian Allan Printing Ltd,
Hersham, Surrey, KT12 4RG

Title page: **The GS&WR branch to Kenmare
was completed in September 1893. This
view, showing a McDonnell 0-4-4T No 39
and its train at the terminus, must have
been taken shortly after its opening, yet
the first two six-wheelers go right back to
the company's early days. The Brake-third
exhibits several features in common with
those on Departmental four-wheeler A24
(see page 9): the 'wrap-over' roof lookout
and style of side and end panelling,
including 'dog-box'. The second coach
appears to be a Composite with central
luggage-boot. Note the dummy 'venetians'
along the top quarters and the five lamp-
tops, but what is the other roof
excrescence? The engine is fitted with
Aspinall's automatic vacuum brake with
necessitated the use of two train pipes, a
feature which probably mitigated against
its general adoption.**
Courtesy, The Green Studio.

CONTENTS

MOBILE ARCHITECTURE

There was a strange period in the mid-twenti-
eth century when railways and all their works
were derided and scoffed at by one body that
should have known better, the architectural
profession. The great railway stations, including the old Euston, were written off as cavernous and soot-encrusted anachronisms that
stank of fish! Similar treatment was given to the
great viaducts of stone or brick or steel that
marched across cities and country landscapes,
when at the same time a new high-level road-
way into London was rhapsodised by a writer
in the architectural press to whom the sight of
'lorries in the sky' was romance par excellence.
Fortunately, attitudes were changing slowly,
partly due to the late Sir John Betjeman, a self-
confessed railway enthusiast and protagonist
for Victorian architecture. One recalls the
Royal Institute of British Architects holding a
post-war conference in Blackpool, and
Howard Robertson, RIBA President at that
time, giving the accolade to the electric tramcars of Blackpool by calling them 'mobile
architecture'. Perhaps that helped to explain
why the present author, who had chosen the
same profession, had a fascination from early
childhood for railway carriages.

The first such conveyances passed before his
infant eyes on the Dublin & South Eastern line
to Kingstown, or Dun Laoghaire as it had
recently been renamed. It was soon apparent
that there was a great variety of coaching stock
on that line, especially around the time of the
amalgamation in 1925. One distinctive vehicle
recently outshopped from Grand Canal Street
works (for it was freshly done up in crimson
lake with the DSER initials) I now realise, was
an open bogie coach that had been converted
from a steam railcar. Others were very old, with
oil lamps that were housed in what to a child
looked like perforated salmon tins on the carriage roofs. Their wheels were spoked, like
goods wagons. There were also large high-
roofed bogie carriages seemingly painted dull
black; these must have been transferred from
the GS&WR that used a purple lake livery
which darkened noticeably with age. Brake
and luggage vans had a special attraction (the
varieties on the Great Southern Railways were
legion), with heavily-barred windows that gave
an air of importance. Of an evening, there were
particular trains to look for; the mail to Dun
Laoghaire Pier with an assortment of through
carriages, mahogany ones from the Great
Northern were most noticeable, but there
must have been examples from the Great
Southern & Western and Midland Great Western as well. Then, if bedtime had been delayed,
there was the chance to see the down Wexford
Mail with its veteran six-wheel sorting van,
complete with net and the strange gold-leaf initials 'P 7 T' in Irish script; what looked like the
figure 7 was the Irish ampersand and it all
stood for [Department of] Posts and
Telegraphs. These TPO vans lasted to be photographed 30 years later.

Railway journeys in those days were usually
local, but the Dun Laoghaire line tended to be
neglected in favour of the Dublin United tram
that were attractive in their own right; a trip on
one of these was often the precursor to a Sun-
day afternoon walk along the East Pier, a seemingly endless expanse of Dalkey granite that
was boredom itself, being completely devoid
of railway tracks. The railway was used on
annual holidays, from Westland Row (Pearse)
to the Pier station at Dun Laoghaire; this was
interesting in itself in having locomotive
turntables at either end of the timber-piled
Carlisle Pier, but there was queasy anticipation
of the sea-crossing, especially if our vessel was
RMS Cambria, whose journeys never seemed
as smooth as those aboard her two sister ships.
The return trip was invariably made at night
and the arrival at Dun Laoghaire in a chill
dawn, followed by the humiliation inflicted by
the Free State Customs, made the last part of
the journey somewhat worse than that on the
night train to Holyhead, which had reasonably
comfortable side-corridor bogie stock. It was
back to Westland Row in a six-wheel Third
whose wooden seats, like church pews, were
trimmed with strips of carpet. 'Boat Train
stock indeed! Nowadays, many of us would
like to sample it again. Nostalgia is a strange
thing.

DEDICATION

In general terms, I would like to dedicate this
book to the anonymous draughtsmen and
craftsmen of the Irish railway carriage building
industry who developed and combined the old
skills of carpentry, cabinet-making, metal
working, painting and glazing to achieve the
high standards of coach-building that are illustrated in these pages. We shall not see their like
again.

In particular, it is dedicated to the memory
of one railway engineer, John Harold Houston
who in his long service with the Northern
Counties Committee of the Midland and LMS
Railways and their successors, combined an
affection for his work with a singular willing-
ness to impart what he had learned to the rank
and file of those fascinated by the subject.

INTRODUCTION

In 1922, the year when the railways of Britain were grouped into four large companies (leaving several minor concerns to fend for themselves) and, more importantly for this narrative, the time of Irish Partition, there were some 26 companies in the Emerald Isle operating their own locomotives and rolling stock. Of these, no less than 14 were narrow (three-foot) gauge, regrettably omitted from the present survey but the subject of a future volume. Yes, there was one other, the ailing Listowel & Ballybunion, but as you all know, this was a monorail and therefore had no gauge at all and expired in 1924. The fledgling administration of the Irish Free State found itself with 13 independent railway undertakings wholly within its jurisdiction in the 26 counties. None of them was in a healthy state. All were debilitated from the privations of World War One and knocked about in the 1916 Insurrection and its aftermath. Worse was to come with the damage inflicted during the civil war that followed in 1922/23. The Free State's answer to such problems was the compulsory amalgamation of these companies. This had been completed by 1925, creating the Great Southern Railways. Notable exceptions had to be made. The Great Northern Railway (Ireland) operated a considerable network that crossed and re-crossed the new border and would become without doubt the most progressive railway in the whole country. Two smaller broad gauge lines also had border crossings, as had the two narrow gauge systems which served County Donegal. So, with seven broad gauge companies amalgamating with six on the narrow gauge, Ireland was to retain its fascinating if uneconomic variety of engines, stock and equipment, spread over ten independent companies that existed precariously until the onset of state ownership in both parts of Ireland. This was fully accomplished by 1958, at the cost of huge gaps in the network.

Before we begin to look at the carriages, let us define the authorities, undertakings and companies that have operated broad (5ft 3in) gauge rolling stock across the 32 counties. The list includes the initials that will be substituted as their story unfolds. Iarnrod Eireann (IE); is the present title of the state owned railway operator in the Irish Republic. IE was preceded by Coras Iompair Eireann (CIE). This was the name of the company formed in 1945 which operated the railways and other public transport in the south. Fully nationalised since 1950, CIE now exists as the holding company controlling IE. The Great Southern Railways (GSR); as has already been mentioned, was formed in 1925 by the amalgamation of all the railway companies wholly located within the 26 counties. The Great Southern & Western Railway (GSWR) had been the largest railway company in Ireland and was the biggest component of the GSR. In the course of its history, it had absorbed several other companies which are referred to in the text. These include, the Waterford Limerick & Western (WLWR), the Waterford Dungarvan & Lismore (WDLR) and the Waterford & Central Ireland Rly (WCIR).

The other major components of the GSR were the Midland Great Western Railway (MGWR) and the Dublin & South Eastern Railway(DSER). This had been known up to 1906 as the Dublin Wicklow & Wexford (DWWR).It operated the Dublin & Kingstown Railway (DKR), Ireland's first line which was leased by DWWR from 1846 though it retained its independent identity until 1925. The GSR also swallowed up the Cork & Macroom Direct Railway (CMDR), the Waterford & Tramore Railway (WTR) and Cork Bandon & South Coast Rly (CBSCR). The latter was an amalgam of local lines in west Cork formed around the Cork & Bandon Railway. This also included the Timoleague & Courtmacsherry Extension Light Railway (TCLR), not surprisingly a very short twig from a CBSCR branch.

It is scarcely necessary to say that the railway network forged by the above companies has been drastically reduced over the past half-century and is now little more than a series of lines radiating from Dublin to the principal provincial centres.

Lines which crossed the border or were located in Northern Ireland were of course excluded from the formation of the GSR. Their fate was rather different. These were led by the Great Northern Railway (Ireland) (GNRI). This was Ireland's second largest railway company, formed in 1876 by amalgamation of the three railways linking Belfast with Dublin the Ulster Railway (UR), the Dublin & Drogheda (DDR) and the Dublin & Belfast Junction (DBJR). To these was added the Irish North Western Rly (INWR), itself a fusion of smaller railways between Dundalk and Derry. Other small railways also came under GNR control in later years. Despite the GNR's plucky efforts to modernise after World War Two, financial failure was averted only by a joint takeover by the two governments in 1953, with a change of name to the Great Northern Railway Board (GNRB), a stop-gap measure largely scuppered by the northern government's insistence on the closure of loss-making lines in its bailiwick. The remains were divided in 1958 between CIE and the Ulster Transport Authority (UTA), previously created to merge the railways located in Northern Ireland with the state-owned Northern Ireland Road Transport Board. After that, little remained of the GNR beyond the Dublin to Belfast main line.

The Belfast & County Down Railway (BCDR) comprised 80 route miles in that north eastern county. Its main line ran from Belfast to Newcastle. The most profitable part of the system was the branch from Belfast to Bangor. This is the only part of the former BCDR network to survive. The BCDR was the UTA's first victim. All of it except the Bangor branch was closed in 1950.

The other major part of Ulster's railway network, with lines to Londonderry, Portrush, Larne and many destinations in mid-Ulster such as Cookstown and Limavady was operated up to 1903 by the Belfast & Northern Counties Railway (BNCR). In that year the BNCR was acquired by the English Midland Railway. Run by local management known as the Northern Counties Committee (NCC), at the British grouping in 1923, this became part of the vast London Midland & Scottish Railway. The management committee was now known as the LMS/NCC. When the LMS became part of the newly nationalised British Railways , the NCC

Left and below: **This is the famous 'Dargan's Saloon' built by Dawson of Phibsboro in Dublin, that became the Midland Great Western's State Carriage. Its rather heavy appearance when viewed broadside is redeemed by the unusual treatment of the coach ends, seen here in 1964, with cracked glass covered in adhesive tape. Its original Dawson built underframe was replaced at Broadstone before the end of the nineteenth century. The interior was also altered during its long career, having lavatory accommodation provided at one time**

Bottom: **These ancient six-wheelers in the Broadstone breakdown train, photographed on 11th April 1950, seem to be precursors of Martin Atock's standard carriages built for the MGWR from 1879 onwards.**

ines were nominally under the control of the British) Railway Executive from 1st January. 948 until they were taken over by the UTA on st April 1949. Predictably, much of the system vas rapidly closed down by its new owners. When the Ulster Transport Authority was bro- ken up in 1968, the few remaining rail services n the province which the UTA had managed not to close, were taken over by Northern Ire- and Railways (NIR). Under NIR capital became vailable for new trains and a new central sta- ion in Belfast. Further reorganisation took place in 1995 when again, rail and road ervices were brought together, UTA style, under the new title of Translink. Once more he railways seem to have been shunted into econd place.

The two other concerns left independent in 925 also fared badly. The Dundalk Newry & Greenore Railway (DNGR) was an Irish broad auge miniature of the London & North West- rn Railway (LNWR), who owned and worked in connection with the Greenore-Holyhead teamer services. Lines ran from Greenore to Newry and Dundalk. Though it became part of he LMS in 1923, it was not managed from Belfast by the NCC as part of it was in a foreign ountry. Run on behalf of the LMS by the GNR, n whose territory it was lodged, from the 930s, it was closed by the British Transport ommission in 1951.The final line to be con- dered was the Sligo Leitrim & Northern ounties Railway (SLNCR) which operated a 2¾ mile single line from the GNR station in nniskillen to a junction with the Sligo line of he MGWR at Collooney. It achieved fame at its osure in 1957 by being the last independent tatutory railway in the United Kingdom. It ent down fighting. Though heavily depend- ent on subsidies for several decades, it was only with the mass closures of GNR lines cen- red on Enniskillen that provided the outlet for s traffic , that it finally succumbed.

Matter of Gauge
he reasons behind the unusual Irish railway auge of 5ft 3in has been told before, but as it ad some effect on carriage design, it is worth mentioning here. The Dublin & Kingstown ine had but one example to copy, the Liver- ool & Manchester Railway of 1830, and it was atural that the D&K adopted the Stephenson auge of 4ft 8½in. So did most of Europe, but he second Irish railway, the Ulster of 1839, ent by the book and sought advice from the hree Railway Commissioners, appointed in 836. These gentlemen were obviously unim- ressed with Stephenson's 'coal cart' gauge ut neither did they go along with Brunel's t 0½in. Their recommendation of a gauge of t 2in was accepted by the Ulster company, ho had built 25 miles to this gauge, from elfast to Portadown by 1842. At the other end f what would eventually become the Dublin- elfast main line, construction of the Dublin & rogheda Railway was by now well advanced, nd it had been expected to lay its track to the me gauge as the Ulster Railway. The D&D

engineer was none other than Sir John Mac- Neill, whose services were sought after by most of the Irish companies of that time. MacNeill does seem to have had a talent for causing strife among his contemporaries, and came up with a gauge of 5ft 2in that had allegedly fig- ured in a report of 1838. The Board of Trade's Inspector-General of Railways was appealed to and looked for a consensus, selecting 5ft 3in as an average between the narrowest (5ft) and broadest (5ft 6in). Thus 5ft 3in was made the lawful Irish railway gauge by an Act of 1846. The UR was justly annoyed, but gauge conver- sion was made relatively easy by laying a 5ft 3in gauge track alongside the existing 6ft 2in track and converting the original line later. Nobody seems to have bothered about the D&K, who would eventually have its tracks widened at the expense of the DWWR. If the European stan- dard gauge had been adopted for Ireland a lot of capital, always in short supply on Irish lines, might have been saved in locomotive and rolling stock manufacture, to say nothing of the possibility of future train ferries, one of Thomas Bouch's better ideas. One running between Larne and Stranraer would have been an obvious example. Had there been a com- mon gauge on both sides of the Irish Sea, there would undoubtedly have been a thriving trade in second-hand rolling stock that might have retarded indigenous Irish railway carriage design to an even greater extent. Had Ireland's railways been operated by castoffs from across the water, this book would never have needed to be written!

Very Early Carriages
There is a certain irony in beginning a review of broad gauge carriages in Ireland by describ- ing the standard gauge coaches of the D&K. Several of these survived to be re-gauged and indeed two open-sided specimens were sent to the centenary celebrations of the Stockton & Darlington Railway in 1925, along with the 1848 GSWR Bury locomotive 2-2-2 No. 36. The remaining one of the pair of D&K coaches is now at the Ulster Folk and Transport Museum in Cultra, County Down. Just as some urban tramway systems retained a handful of open- topped cars for summer use, some open-sided 'Kingstowns' were kept by the DWWR literally in the basement of Grand Canal Street works and were hauled into daylight every summer for excursion trips to the seaside. They were roofed four-wheelers with sides open above the waist and both underframes and bodies were considerably narrower than the later car- riages. Some were glazed on one side only. Their footboards were extra wide, and were put to uses which would have horrified the present Health and Safety profession. Other- wise, carriage bodies on the D&K were con- ventional, First and Second class examples being an amalgam, of stage coach bodies from which evolved the compartment coach familiar to later generations. Third class carriages were open above the waist and minus doors, resem- bling the 'toastrack' tramcars that appeared in

seaside towns a generation or two later. How- ever, they were roofed and the ends were enclosed, while canvas blinds were later affixed to the seaward side of some Thirds. The survivors already referred to were believed to have been 'open' Seconds originally.

Dublin since the eighteenth century had developed a fine reputation for coachbuilding, so there was no need to look far for carriage bodies, though the first underframes and run- ning gear were supplied by English builders, as were some of the open Thirds. Others of this ilk came from Courtney and Stephens of Dublin, a firm which later branched out into signalling equipment and general railway hardware. Fifty coaches were ordered for the opening of the D&K in 1834, forming five trains each of one First class, four Second class and three Third class carriages, with 10 vehi- cles spare. The most notable of local suppliers to the first Irish railways was the Dublin firm of J S Dawson of Phibsborough, later Dawson, Rogerson and Russell. They were out of busi- ness by the early 1860s, largely due to the commencement of 'in-house' coach-building by the principal railways, including the D&K when their Grand Canal Street works had been fitted out. One guesses that many skilled tradesmen were poached from private builders.

The D&K soon began to build six-wheeled carriages; the original four-wheeled Firsts had been replaced by 1843 and 'cascaded' to Sec- ond class, while some Thirds were useful for conversion to Brake vans. Presumably with the foreknowledge that conversion of its tracks to 5ft 3in gauge was inevitable, the Kingstown company was soon building wide-bodied stock seating four-a-side in the First class and six-a- side in Seconds and Thirds. The leasing agree- ment in 1856 (coinciding with the D&K's change of gauge) brought 86 Kingstown coach- ing vehicles, wide and narrow, under DWWR control. These consisted of 9 First class, 38 Sec- ond class, 20 Third class, 10 'Atmospheric' coaches (4 Seconds and 6 Thirds) from the Dalkey Extension built to Brunel's ill-fated design, a State Carriage and 8 parcels and Mail vans. The State Carriage was the first of its kind in Ireland, being converted from a new 4-com- partment First in 1849 for Queen Victoria's ini- tial visit to Ireland. It was approximately 23ft 6in long, with a central saloon (11ft 5in), a vestibule at one end and a compartment for ladies-in-waiting at the other. This first State Carriage was withdrawn in 1894. One further feature of D&K coach design that is said to have been perpetuated up to change of gauge, may well have been unique. This was the central buffer/coupling invented by one of the D&K's supervisory staff, T F Bergin. It was to provide a stress-free underframe by having a central drawbar that projected about three feet beyond the coach headstock and ended in a circular buffer-face, coupled to its neighbour by hooks and chains. There is a detailed description of this by K A Murray in his defin- itive history of the D&K, *Ireland's First Railway* (IRRS, 1981).

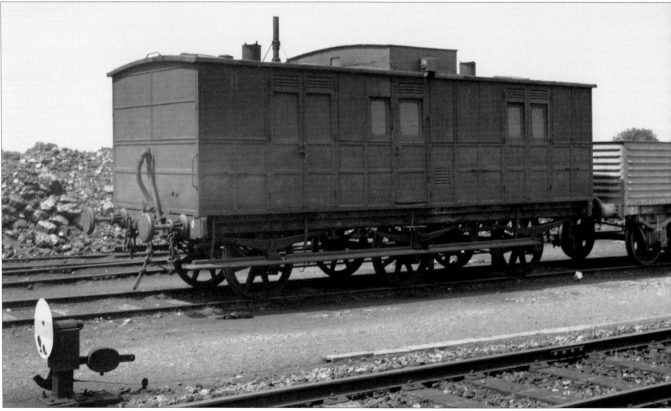

Top: **This early McDonnell Luggage-first-second No 518, built in 1879, seen here on 2nd June 1951, was later converted to Sleeping car No 235A for use by Permanent Way staff. Roof tanks to provide a water supply and a handbrake have been added. The vehicle is painted in CIE passenger livery.**

Above: **Some vehicles of very great vintage could still be seen in service on the CIE network in the 1960s. This ex-G&SWR main line passenger van, numbered 15A, dating from the 1850s was in use as the Thurles breakdown van when photographed on 4th June 1961. Even as** late as this a complete train of ancient carriages could have been gathered together from outlying CIE locomotive sheds. If only the preservation movement had taken off sooner

Let us briefly glance at some of the other early Irish railways. The Ulster Railway had taken second place opening between Belfast and Lisburn on 12th August 1839. Its first four carriages, believed to be English built and conveying First and Second-class passengers only, were considered sufficient to work a shuttle service over seven miles of track; nor did there seem to be any need for Third class accommodation until the line had reached Lurgan in 1841. Third class then took the form of high-sided open wagons without seats which lasted until the end of 1856. The Dublin & Drogheda Railway introduced the 5ft 3in gauge to Ireland when it opened on 24th May 1844. No detailed description of its coaching stock seems to have survived, but J S Dawson's factory had risen to the occasion and provided upwards of a score of six-wheeled Firsts and Composites for opening day. Seatless but roofed Third class carriages came from another local firm, Messrs Adams. During the 1840s the main line of the GSWR was being driven south-west towards the city of Cork, while the Waterford & Limerick had already cut across its right-of-way at the famous flat crossing at Limerick Junction, opening its line from Limerick to Tipperary on 9th May 1848. The GSWR opened its main line to a temporary Cork terminus, short of the tunnel, that would take it to the present Glanmire Road (now Kent) station, on 29th October 1849.

Technology had advanced by leaps and bounds in the 15 years since the D&K had opened. This was the first Irish trunk railway and the GSWR was wealthy enough to benefit from the improvement in engineering practice and design which had occurred since the opening of the D&K. Today, we look at its buildings, those stations that have survived, from Kingsbridge (Heuston) terminus, whose exterior once inspired Hamilton Ellis to muse upon what railways might have been like if they had been invented in the days of Inigo Jones, past the older part of Inchicore works (Ellis thought this as good as Balliol College in Oxford) and all the exquisitely-detailed wayside stations in cut limestone, to that strange oasis of Limerick Junction with its massive (from rail-level anyway) hotel block giving an impression of civilised security in the heart of primeval Gaeldom. But, apart from No 36, the 1847 Bury built 2-2-2 on its plinth in Cork's Glanmire Road station, we must imagine the first locomotives and trains that served this line, though some ancient photographs have survived. The carriages especially were a step forward from previous examples. They were mainly six-wheeled. First class coaches had four compartments with an oil lamp to each and they seated four persons aside. Seconds had five compartments; the wooden seats held five aside and partitions stopped short of the ceiling, allowing two oil lamps to illuminate the entire interior. This was somewhat better than Third class where the six compartments had seat backs stopping a mere 18in above posterior level and night journeys were made

in total darkness for the first few years. All carriages were on a standard underframe 26ft long, as were the Brake vans. The latter had 'birdcage' roof-lookouts with an elevated seat for the Guard.

Even a century ago, cynics denied that six-wheelers had any virtue, giving passengers three jolts per rail-joint rather than a mere two in a four-wheeler. Despite this, Joseph Tatlow, who came to Ireland to manage the BCDR in 1885, paid the Irish railways a compliment when he noticed that six-wheelers were the norm on Irish long-distance trains when English passengers had to put up with a greater proportion of four-wheeled coaches. Carriage heating was unheard-of in those formative years.

Local coachbuilders such as Dawson led the field in providing the first carriages for the GSWR, after which Inchicore works was equipped for coach-building on a regular basis. Dawson also contributed to the coaching stock of the MGWR, which opened its main line to Galway as far as Enfield in County Meath on 26th June 1847. It was very likely a Dawson vehicle that Sir Francis Head described in his book, *A Fortnight in Ireland* (1852), quoted at length in E Shepherd's, *Midland Great Western Railway of Ireland* (Midland Publishing 1994). Head found himself in a very elegant First class coupé' having such ample headroom, he could walk around with his hat on! A sliding door divided the coupé (when required) into two compartments, and a cloth-covered table under the plate-glass end windows concealed two folding beds and their mattresses. A First class ticket or two on the night mail to Galway must have provided some enjoyment, provided one's personal timetable was well planned. It also should be noticed that in those days the MGWR provided a Fourth class of conveyance, sketchily converting open cattle wagons for the purpose and retaining the right to re-convert them when required.

By the time the MGWR, known in Ireland simply as 'the Midland', commenced business in 1847, its contractor William Dargan, was also active all over the country on other railway projects. To get around these, Dargan had a personal saloon made by Dawson. He later presented this to the MGWR and it has survived to occupy an honoured place at the Ulster Folk and Transport Museum, as the last remaining example of Dawson's craftsmanship. Dargan was particularly busy in Ulster where he had secured contracts for building both the Belfast & Ballymena and Belfast & County Down railways, the former opening its line on 11th April 1848 and the BCDR following suit with its Holywood branch on 2nd August. The late Harold Houston, who spent his working life with the Northern Counties Committee in Belfast and contributed much to what we know of the BNCR's history, recorded that a proportion of the B&B's original rolling stock including 4-wheel and 6-wheel carriages, was built by Thomas Firth. Firth was a Yorkshire-

man who had established a factory on the Falls Road in Belfast and was mainly engaged in wagon building. The B&B examples are the only known carriages built by Firth. They probably included the open, wooden seated Thirds (roofed in 1856) that would have been well within a wagon builder's scope. Mr Houston, in his paper (*IRRS Journal No 35, 1964*) also mentions First and Second class carriages built in England for the B&BR. The BCDR's initial carriages came from Joseph Wright, whose works were still apparently based in London when the order was placed, well in advance of the railway's completion. Wright's factory in Saltley, Birmingham, supplied six First class and 12 Second class carriages, all 4-wheelers. No significant increase in stock took place until the main line was extended to Downpatrick in 1858/9. The reconstituted firm of Rogerson, Dawson and Russell supplied a sizeable (for the BCDR) quantity of carriages and wagons, including four First class 6-wheelers. The remainder, Composites, Seconds and Horseboxes had four wheels. The BCDR was another company to start by only offering First and Second class seats. Third class appeared when old Seconds were converted for the extension in 1858. The Wright coaches lasted over-long with this impecunious company. Four of them were offered for sale in 1878. The DWWR was interested and sent its Locomotive Superintendent to inspect. He was not impressed by what he saw, but he has given us the only written description of these 1848 carriages.

'They were made by Mr Jos. Wright of London, supplied when the railway was made over 25 years ago. They are a very old type, small size and very low roofs, so low passengers must take off their hats or stoop well down when they enter the carriages. [Headgear was still important in 1878!]. *There are two sets of wheels to each. Nos 1, 2 and 3 have four compartments to carry 32 passengers. No 5 is the same description but has been altered to a saloon with two compartments of equal size.*

Taking a quick look at the Waterford & Limerick, Ireland's first provincial railway (if we except the Ulster as being earmarked from the first as part of the Dublin-Belfast trunk route), we find from 1848 to 1859, a large quantity of 6-wheeled stock by a variety of builders including Dawson, Fagan, Wright, Hutton and Kinder, though there was one important difference that puts the W&L in the vanguard of British railway companies, in that it was the first user of bogie carriages. The W&L engineer, one Richard Osborne, what Irish folk call, a 'returned Yank'. He had learnt his profession on the Philadelphia & Reading Railroad, and while he was a Civil Engineer, he had a 'master mechanic' in charge of the company's Limerick workshops, supervising construction of a quantity of Third class bogie cars of typical American design around 1847. It seems that the W&L directorate were too hide-bound to accept this transatlantic innovation. Osborne returned to the USA and his bogie railroad cars were sawn in half and rebuilt as 4-wheel Brake vans. From then on, the W&L followed convention and ordered carriages from Ashbury, Metropolitan (as Jos. Wright had become) and other large concerns, as well as maintaining a regular output from their own works. Bogie stock did not come again until the 1890s, just before the WLWR was swallowed up by the GSWR.

Depopulation and economic depression made for painfully slow growth during a great part of the nineteenth century. Locally funded branch lines often teetered on the verge of bankruptcy before being 'saved' by a large company at the expense of the original shareholders. Various palliatives were considered. A report of 1868 advocated state ownership of Irish railways. It did not, apparently, arouse either Treasury concern or public worry about

taxation, the United Kingdom as a whole was enjoying a growing prosperity, better founded than the sort we enjoy today, but the idea was simply allowed to fade away. A body of informed opinion at the present time might well say, 'what a pity it never happened then.' One feature of that report of interest to the historian was a mass of statistical information on all the Irish railways, both built and authorised. The following table showing the coaching stock owned by individual companies was included:

Class Distinctions
James Allport of the Midland Railway made his mark on British railway history by taking the unimagined step of abolishing Second class in 1875. At the same time, as Hamilton Ellis has

said, 'Allport comforted the third class traveller with cushions', a move which was even more upsetting to the other companies, as they were bound, however grudgingly, to follow suit. It was a long drawn out affair and Second class lingered on some London suburban services for many years. Indeed because of the continental attachment to three classes of accommodation, it survived on certain boat-train services up to nationalisation in 1948. For various social and economic reasons, Second class travel in Ireland proved much harder to eradicate. The first major Irish company to break the habit was the MGWR in 1914, while the newly formed Great Southern Railways, perpetuating GSWR practice, did not take the plunge until 1930.

Having taken as gospel what he had read in the railway histories then available to young folk, the author recalls his surprise on finding that the doors of those distinctive mahogany carriages at rest in Amiens Street (Connolly) station were proudly lettered, in gold leaf of course, for all three classes. Not only the GNR had ignored Allport's dictum, for Second class was flourishing on all the northern lines, even on the Midland's successor, the LMS. Admittedly, Second class had more of a token presence on their Northern Counties lines. Compartments in the newer rolling stock were identical in length and upholstery to Third class. Other companies applied a firm yardstick to compartment length, the knee room increasing proportionally to the fare charged. The BCDR had avoided trimming its Thirds until the more enlightened GNR penetrated its Newcastle stronghold in 1906. But it had to end sometime. The GNR announced abolition of Second class with effect from 1st January 1951. At the same time, First class fares were reduced. Third class officially became Second class on 3rd June 1956, as it had in Britain. CIE soon renamed its Second class as Standard class and British Railways eventually followed suit, though with the decline in First class travel the expression is hardly heard nowadays. Another irony was that the last part of the Irish railway system to see genuine Second class was that outpost of the old Midland empire, the NCC, by now run by the UTA. The BCDR section had lost its right to Second class when steam traction on the Bangor line was abolished in 1953. The replacement railcars catered only for First and Third. First class in these was soon dispensed with. Nowadays in Northern Ireland, only the cross-border services of Translink cater for First class passengers.

Definitions
Roof contour is a convenient way of identifying and dating old railway carriages. The earliest were roofed with a very slight camber, when it was commonplace to carry passengers' baggage on coach roofs. Experience led to the provision of luggage compartments in Brake vans and carriages, while the radius of camber was progressively decreased as internal headroom

From the Report of the Railways (Ireland) Commission, May 1868

'* These companies, which are not listed in the Introduction, are respectively: Belfast Holywood & Bangor (opened 1865, absorbed by BCDR 1884); Cork Blackrock & Passage (converted to 3-foot gauge 1900); Dublin & Meath (worked by the MGWR from 1869 until absorption in 1889), Londonderry & Lough Swilly (converted to 3-foot gauge in 1885), Newry & Armagh (absorbed by the GNR(I) in 1879); Newry, Warrenpoint & Rostrevor (absorbed by the GNR(I) 1886); Waterford & Kilkenny renamed Waterford & Central Ireland (absorbed by the GSWR 1900), West Cork Railway, amalgamated with the Cork & Bandon in 1880, the whole becoming the Cork Bandon & South Coast Railway in 1888.'

Anomalies in the table below can be seen, caused by interpretation by the individuals who furnished the returns. For example, Passenger Brake vans invariably had luggage accommodation, and a large number of Luggage vans carried Guards and had brakes. We know that the first two companies in the table both had Brake vans that carried luggage. But then the BHBR was a quirky concern, despite what the report says, it did carry Third class passengers!

CARRIAGE STOCK AT 30TH JUNE 1867

	First Class	Second Class	Third Class	Composite	Luggage Vans	Mail & Sorting Vans	Horseboxes	Carriage Trucks	State Carriages	Pass. Brake Vans	Total Stock
BCDR	9	7	12	16	8	–	3	–	–	–	55
* BHBR	18	23	–	5	–	–	–	–	–	4	50
BNCR	11	6	40	36	–	–	10	8	–	14	125
C&BR (CBSCR)	1	–	7	5	–	–	2	4	–	5	24
* CB&PR	3	2	6	2	–	–	–	–	–	2	15
CMDR	2	3	4	–	–	–	–	–	–	2	11
D&BJR	7	6	12	10	6	–	10	10	–	–	61
D&DR	8	10	24	21	–	–	12	12	–	12	99
* D&MR	2	6	10	4	–	–	6	–	–	1	29
DWWR	27	60	50	6	20	2	6	4	–	–	175
GS&WR	68	54	82	25	42	12	52	30	1	–	366
INWR	–	4	23	26	25	–	8	8	–	–	94
LLSR	–	–	4	2	–	–	–	–	–	–	7
MGWR	3	9	54	47	25	–	38	22	1	–	199
* N&AR	2	1	4	5	–	–	2	1	–	3	18
* NW&RR	3	3	3	–	1	–	–	–	–	–	10
Ulster Rly	14	12	31	14	20	3	10	5	–	–	109
* W&KR	6	11	6	6	3	–	4	2	–	–	38
W&LR (WL&WR)	7	6	21	12	–	–	9	7	–	9	71
W&TR	6	–	7	1	–	–	–	–	–	1	15
* West Cork Rly	1	–	6	4	–	–	2	2	–	2	17
	198	223	406	247	150	17	174	115	2	56	1588

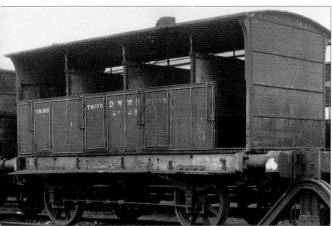

Top: **The train shed at Waterford Manor Station may have been an impediment to photography but did help in prolonging the life of rolling stock on the Waterford & Tramore line. Henry Casserley's picture taken on 14th September 1929 is, except for the humanity, an absolute time-warp. Nothing later than 1850s is seen apart from the second-hand Dungarvan carriage partly visible on right. Two Dawson Firsts occupy centre stage. The nearest one is the 'bed-carriage' to be described later, and the furthermost vehicle is one of the unglazed specimens modelled on the early Dublin & Kingstown Railway stock.** H C Casserley.

Above left: **One of the Kingstown open Thirds that was done up for the 1925 centenary celebrations is seen on the Inchicore dump. It was rescued many years later, needing quite a lot of new woodwork, and sent to what was then the Belfast Transport Museum. It is now part of the Irish Railway Collection at the Ulster Folk & Transport Museum at Cultra near Belfast. Part of another open, even older and quainter, is also seen, but years of exposure to the elements put paid to that one.** H C Casserley.

Above right: **Still bearing its GS&WR Departmental number A24, this black liveried four-wheel Brake van of the 1850s has made its final journey to Inchicore. Its last assignment had been 'Limerick Junction Tool Van' and judging from its good external condition, it must have spent much of its time there inside the engine shed. Seen on 27th March 1951, it had scarcely altered in nearly a century of service, save for the addition of footboards and vacuum pipes.**

became more important. With the development of the 'elliptical' section (half-elliptical is more accurate but cumbersome) the older profile became known as 'flat'. In these pages, the terminology of the GNR will be followed where practicable; flat (F), low-elliptical (LE), clerestory (C) and high-elliptical (HE) but there are variations. Some companies, notably the GSWR, reduced the radius of the curve to a marked extent, qualifying it for the term 'segmental' which the writer prefers to 'arcroofed', an expression that seems to be popular among the modelling fraternity. The DSER favoured a contour on its later carriages that was parabolic.

Apart from purely passenger-carrying vehicles, coaching stock included in this survey qualifies by having longer bearing springs (around 6ft for rigid wheelbase vehicles), oil axleboxes and larger journals, screw couplings and carriage-type buffers and drawgear. Exceptions are axiomatic; occasional goods vehicles were rated for use in passenger trains. The statistical table of 1867 includes the standard types that were codified by the Board of Trade for the half-yearly returns that each company was expected to furnish. This practice continued up to the year 1912. The last half-yearly returns were dated 31st December 1912. Thereafter, returns were annual, the criterion being the number of seats in the respective classes. In the old format, every type and class of vehicle was catered for, though the term 'Composite' was ambiguous. In the beginning it is safe to assume that only First and Second class compartments were involved. With the increasing length of 6-wheeled stock, coach designers began to ring the changes, and the culmination was the Tri-composite ('Trio' in railway parlance). Another anomaly arose with Brake-ended coaches (these too could be Trios) that managed to avoid classification but became widespread when bogie stock was introduced.

Carriage braking was largely non-existent, apart from those on Brake vans themselves. It was augmented at first by putting a Brakesman outside, with a seat on the roof-end. Soon enough, the poor wretch was allowed a seat in an ordinary compartment; this was the beginning of the Brake-ended coach mentioned previously and one recalls Guards sharing their domain with the public on some bogie coaches of the Isle of Man Railway. Continuous brakes were engaging inventors' ingenuity at an early date and usually involved knuckle-jointed connections or chains between coaches. Newall's patent brake was tried on the BCDR and probably elsewhere in Ireland. When vacuum brakes came into use Smith's non-automatic brake was popular, with tragic results in the Armagh runaway of 1889. A quick parliamentary response outlawed all but automatic continuous brakes and vacuum braking in that manner became the rule in Ireland. On the GSWR Aspinall's vacuum brake was used. E L Ahrons illustrates its principle in Vol. 6 of *Locomotive and Train Working in the latter part of the l9th Century*. Aspinall found a way of making Smith s brake automatic and this was modified by the Vacuum Brake Company to produce the automatic brake that was standard in the United Kingdom and Ireland until recently. But the Smith's brake was to cause further mischief. It remained in use on the SLNCR, a distant backwater, until a seriocomic buffer-stop collision on the DNGR brought the Sligo company's disregard of the law to light in 1904. Four of its coaches were the leading vehicles in a train entering Greenore terminus, so that nothing happened when the engine driver used his brake, a collision with the buffer stop being the inevitable conclusion. The Westinghouse air-brake took longer to establish itself in Ireland; the first example that comes to mind was its use on the GNR's electric tramway at Howth in County Dublin. The air-brake re-emerged with the development of diesel multiple unit railcars on the UTA in the early 1950s.

Carriage heating was unheard of on the early railways. Foot-warmers were a mid-nineteenth century invention. These were flat-bottomed hot-water bottles made of tinplate obtainable at the principal stations for a small fee. A travelling rug was also often a necessity, and the larger companies offered these for hire. Steam heating, piped from the locomotive, was not commonplace in Ireland until the twentieth century. Following the demise of steam traction, large amounts of money were poured into a quest for a satisfactory substitute for this, as we shall see later. Carriage lighting was for many years supplied by the oil lamp, rape-seed oil (Colza) and paraffin were used. Oil-gas lighting became popular in the 1890s. The GS&WR was a pioneer of this type of lighting. However, when the GSWR took over the WLWR in 1901, it converted almost new electrically-lit WLWR stock to gas-lighting, a truly retrograde step. In the north, the GNR was proud of the fact that it made a straightforward change from oil to electricity from 1894.

Among other definitions used in the pages which follow, the word 'ducket' has become popular among carriage fanciers as meaning a Guard's side look-out, but one doubts that it was ever used by railwaymen in Ireland. It is a (British) north-country dialect word, derived from 'doocot', meaning dovecote and described the roof look-out of earlier days, sometimes known as a 'bird-cage' which was adopted at one time or another by most Irish railways. The side look-out was referred to as the 'outlook'. The term 'ogee' was often applied to it on the NCC. It was known as a 'cab' on the GNR and as a 'side hood' on the Southern. A hood on CIE otherwise meant a corridor connection, as in the term 'hooded vans'. But we are sure the list can be added to.

Gangways or corridor connections appear to have been associated with postal trains from early times but did not come into general use until Dining cars were made accessible to all classes of passenger. It was then necessary to off-set the gangways on postal sorting vans to thwart potential mail train robbers by making these vehicles inaccessible from the rest of the train. 'V' for vestibule was a handy abbreviation used by the GNR, though possibly inaccurate as the reader will find its other use in these pages as meaning an enclosed lobby the width of a coach, but not always at the ends. The term 'Centre-corridor' is frequently applied to an open coach with a centre gangway or aisle. In the days when virtually all coaches are open it no longer has the Dublin & Kingstown connotation that conjures up damp sea air and the aroma of Merrion Strand at low tide.

Acknowledgments
A representative selection of photographs could not have been assembled, neither could the information on individual companies have been filled out, without the willing help of other railway historians, collectors and photographers. My sincere thanks go to Chris Aspinwall, Gerry Beesley, Roger Carpenter, R M Casserley, Andrew Crockart, Colm Flanagan, C P Friel, Norman Johnston, Sean Kennedy, Robin Linsley, Norman Mc Adams, A H Miles, P Millard, Donal Murray, Herbert Richards, R C Riley, J W P Rowledge and Derek Young. Thanks are also due to Iarnrod Eireann for permission to reproduce the photographs of their de Dietrich carriages and to Tom Ferris of Midland Publishing for his support and encouragement. To those whose names have been inadvertently omitted, my humble apologies. All photographs in the book, not attributed to others, were taken by the author.

Further information on the coaching stock of individual concerns may be found in other Midland Publishing books, namely Ernie Shepherd's *Midland Great Western Railway*, The *Dublin & South Eastern* (Shepherd and Beesley), this writer's *Belfast & County Down Railway, An Irish Railway Pictorial* and Mark Kennedy's, *The LMS In Ireland*.

GSWR Carriage Diagrams (Transport Research Associates, 1975) by Pender and Richards, is another invaluable reference source as is the *Journal of the Irish Railway Record Society*, which since its inception has published many members' papers containing valuable information on the carriages of the GNR, GSR, CIE, MGWR, W&T, BCDR, NCC and other companies as well as those on specialist activities like mail trains, Restaurant cars and Royal trains. The late Michael Harris' definitive *British Rail Mark Two Coaches* shows our indebtedness to the last flowering of British coach design before BR's forced surrender to international big business.

THE GREAT SOUTHERN & ITS CONSTITUENTS

Part of the Rosslare Boat Train at Glanmire Road resplendent in the new GSR (almost Great Western) brown and cream livery. The three clerestories are all from the original rake of 1906/7. From left are, 66ft side-corridor composite No 871 (seven Third and three First class compartments), the 57ft 6in long 12-wheel dining car No 353 (12 First and 22 Third class seats) and 66ft long Brake-composite No 875 (with five Third class compartments comfortably placed in the middle, two First class over one bogie and the van over the other). The roof boards are lettered, 'Through carriage Cork and Rosslare Harbour'. The Green Studio.

In this chapter we will firstly examine some of the carriages of the constituent companies which were amalgamated in 1925 to form the GSR. This will be followed by a look at the relatively small range of vehicles which that company turned out itself. In his naivety, the author once asked an Inchicore man what the GSR Carriage Diagram book was like. The reply was, 'about a foot thick'. It was scarcely an exaggeration, for there was tremendous variety in the rolling stock contributed by the amalgamated companies. Because of necessity, many were vehicles of considerable antiquity - but lovingly maintained, just the same. In 1925, the GSR adopted an interesting method of identifying its carriages. The new concern being the GSWR writ large, the rolling stock of the senior constituent retained their original numbers. The small amount of new construction that followed was given room in the same list. Carriages and wagons of the remaining

companies also kept their own numbers prefixed with a 'section letter'. Only the broad gauge companies are listed below, the absorbed narrow gauge lines having their own letters.

B - Cork Bandon & South Coast
M - Midland Great Western
D - Dublin & South Eastern
J - Timoleague & Courtmacsherry
R - Cork & Macroom
W - Waterford & Tramore

The letter A was reserved for Departmental stock. This system was retained by CIE and amplified in 1958 when the Great Northern was rent in twain. Rolling stock from that company received the suffix 'N', with the strange proviso that coaching stock (but not horse-boxes) had also a prefix 'C'; one supposed it stood for carriage.

GREAT SOUTHERN & WESTERN RAILWAY

Give or take a few blank numbers in its list, the largest railway company in Ireland brought about 895 coaching vehicles into the expanded organisation. There were 235 bogie coaches and 434 six-wheelers. On four wheels, there were 117 horseboxes, 51 ventilated vans for perishable traffic, 32 carriage trucks (another two were six-wheeled) and a further 18 miscellaneous vehicles.

On the retirement of Henry Corlett, carriage and wagon superintendent at Inchicore in 1877, rolling stock became the responsibility of the Locomotive Superintendent, Alexander McDonnell. The latter produced a number of prototype six-wheeled carriages in 1879 that were built in quantity up to the end of the century. Most GSWR six wheelers that survived to 1925 and beyond bore the McDonnell stamp. Top quarters, windows, droplights and waist panels had rounded corners and roof profile was moderately low. A standard length of 30ft over headstocks was adopted for four-compartment Firsts and Saloons, Composites with lavatory accommodation for main line use alternating with Composites having central luggage compartments, Second class with five compartments, Third class and Brake (three compartments), six-compartment Thirds and more than 50 Brake vans with side-lookouts and roof 'birdcages'. There were also a few oddities such as Family saloons.

The first GSWR bogie carriage was a 45ft Lavatory-composite built in 1885, near the end of Aspinall's regime. The prototype was followed between 1888 and 1901 by a further seven of similar dimensions. The layout was altered to allow Second class passengers access to a lavatory and No 507 seems to have been rebuilt to the same plan. The roof profile of these coaches was raised to about 12ft over rail level in the 'segmental' mode. These early lavatory vehicles were easily identifiable by their roof-mounted storage cisterns. Third class bogie carriages began to appear in 1897, eight compartments being crammed into the 45ft length. There was a little more leg-room when the length was increased to 47ft in 1909, but a seven compartment design using the old underframe length had appeared in 1900.

Restaurant cars were introduced in both directions on the Dublin-Cork Day Mails in 1898. The cars were in pairs connected by a gangway and they had clerestory roofs, a status symbol on the GSWR. The Second-class cars had dining space for 24, the remainder of the 45ft underframe being occupied by non-dining accommodation arranged in 'semi-open' fashion, and two lavatories. The kitchen was at one end of the First class restaurant, which seated 14. At the other end was a single First class compartment with an adjoining lavatory, in car No 343 only. That end of No 344 had what appeared to be a wasteful lounge section, for the diagram shows it with only four swivelling armchairs. The Murray/McNeill history of the GSWR (IRRS, 1976) tells us that a third coach was included in each set, a 45ft open First advertised as a 'Drawing Room Car'. The arrangement lasted but two years. Were these three carriages originally isolated from the rest of the train? It had been thus in early days, when those intending to have a meal must perforce remain in the dining car for their entire journey. If there were two sittings on the Day Mail it would account for the additional accommodation for both classes.

A further spur towards excellence was the opening of the direct Rosslare-Cork boat-train service in 1906, for which sets of 66ft vestibuled clerestory stock were provided; these catered for First and Third class only. Of the two restaurant cars, No 353 was a twelve-wheeler 57ft 6in long. No 876 was 66ft long on four wheel bogies, a record for Ireland. The remaining Rosslare clerestories were all First-third side-corridor, stock, three of them being twelve-wheelers with brake compartment.

Underframe length was increased to 57ft during the early 1900s and the first high-elliptical roofed stock came out in 1914. Construction was continued through the war years, adding a further 36 side-corridor 57-footers to stock, mostly Third class but including two dining cars and two side-corridor Tricomposites. A pair of bogie Post Office vans were built in 1919. From then on, Inchicore works resumed building main line side-corridor stock, as well as a batch of handsome bogie Brakes, and was still building to GSWR designs after formation of the Great Southern Railways.

The 'singletons' produced by carriage departments are often the most interesting. First of the line was the original State Carriage built in 1851 (see page 3), to be on hand when required by the Lord Lieutenant. It had a 27ft 10in body on six wheels. Refurbished for Queen Victoria's visit in 1861, and several times after that, it carried the Prince of Wales from time to time (including visits to race meetings), but was past its best when he came to the throne as Edward VII in 1901. For the Royal tour of Ireland that took place in 1903 a new and luxurious State Carriage was built at Inchicore, a 50ft clerestory-roofed vehicle that had a long life, rebuilt and renovated several times. It was given a high-elliptical roof in the 1920s and looked very up to date in the 1950s when mounted on a pair of Commonwealth bogies that were being used for the new CIE stock then being built.

There was less pomp about the two 4-wheeled mortuary vans Nos 708 and 709 of 1882, but they no doubt helped to provide a

One of the pioneer clerestory dining cars of 1898, No 344, whose length over body was 45ft. This was an all First vehicle with an end kitchen in which oil-gas was used for cooking. It ran with a trailer car which served Second class passengers.
The Green Studio.

Right: **Four-compartment First No 302 was built in 1884 on a standard 30ft underframe. Originally gas-lit of course, it lasted until 1959.**

Below: **Lavatory-composite No 540, of similar vintage to No 302, had vanished from GS&WR stock by 1924, but other similar vehicles survived to see service under CIE. Note that although the roof is 'flat', the lavatory cistern, normally very prominent at roof level, is not visible.** Both, The Green Studio.

dignified send-off for many an honest citizen. They were smaller than others in the country, being only 15ft 6in long, unglazed and with central double doors. The ends had ample, louvred ventilation. Strangest of all was No 240, the vehicle bluntly labelled 'hearse' It was dated 1906 and the height from floor to roof was only 3ft 9in. Length and wheelbase (9ft) were the same as the mortuary vans. Was it kept in case there was a multiple tragedy, even a serious accident on the line itself?

On a more cheerful note, Nos 908 and 936 were coupé-ended Composite six-wheelers built in 1896 and were useful conveyances for racegoers. No 936 was kept at Leopardstown. These had a double-door luggage 'boot' inboard of the Second class coupé, while the other Second class had its own lavatory, parallel to that of the First class, whose coupe communicated directly with the main compartment. Another odd vehicle was the saloon No 462 of 1898, also six-wheeled and laid out on Family saloon lines. Between this saloon and the coach end was a full-width lavatory compartment with a curious cupboard. At the other end a side corridor led to a 6-seater First class compartment. Next to this, and possibly connected to the corridor (though no

door is shown) was a half-compartment Second class, seating five. A rather narrow luggage boot with undersized double doors completed the layout. The curious thing about the saloon proper was that it had a pair of unequal-sized double doors on either side, about 3ft in total width. One thinks of an invalid saloon, but it was rated to seat 10, with 6 others in the adjoining section. Both the above types had 30ft bodies on the standard l9ft 2in wheelbase. Sadly, No 462 was broken up in 1927, a short life for a GSWR coach.

Two more 'singletons' are worthy of brief mention. The first known use of a clerestory roof on a GSWR carriage was in 1878, when a First class six-wheeler so equipped was built for use on the Up night mail. Sleeping berths replaced seats in its four compartments, at an extra charge of half a crown (12½ pence) per berth. The object of the clerestory was to provide daylight for occupants to dress by while the droplights and quarterlights were decently curtained. The coach, No 332, had to find its way back to Cork during the day. The experiment was short lived but No 332 had a long career as a normal First, later Third, and finished up on the Leopardstown race specials, being withdrawn in 1954. A better-known

example was the official Inspection car of 1912. It was 42ft long with platforms at each end and a segmental roof. Each platform gave access to a saloon. Amidships was a small compartment where meals could be prepared, and a lavatory. No 352 retained its original purple-lake livery and crest until CIE had taken over. It was withdrawn somewhat prematurely in 1964 after a minor collision.

The WLWR coaching vehicles received numbers between 900 and 1055 in the GSWR list. The passenger stock was mostly six-wheel but included six bogie coaches, two Third class by Ashbury of Manchester and two Composites by the Metropolitan Carriage and Wagon Company, the, successors to Joseph Wright. These were all built in 1896. The bodies were around 48ft in length, as were those of the final pair, built at Limerick works in 1898 with two Second and two Third class compartments and a long section for the Guard and luggage. All six lasted into CIE days and one of the Metropolitan pair was rebuilt as a First class saloon. It ended its days as the 'Radio Train' car, a popular 1950s money-spinner for CIE where the railbound version of disc-jockeys played records and interviewed passengers on these special excursions.

Opposite page:

Top: **Mail sorting at night needed good illumination, hence the profusion of oil lamps on Post Office Van No 139. It is thought that the little flue-pipe to the right of the doors was for a spirit lamp that softened sealing wax, once so important for registered mail. This van ran from 1890 to 1959. The Green Studio.**

Centre: **Built in 1884 as a First-second composite, 30ft over body, six-wheeler No 300 is seen at Limerick Junction on 26th March 1951, three years before withdrawal.**

Bottom: **The 'blank' side of six-wheel TPO 140 looks well with its original panelling intact. It was recorded at Boston Sidings, Westland Row, on 4th April 1953.**

This page:

Below: **Built in 1889 and not withdrawn until 1956, Brake-third No 36 was in surprisingly good order when seen on menial duties on the centre road at Bray on 10th April 1950. Note the belt-and-braces provision of side and roof lookouts.**

Bottom: **Clerestory Brake-tricomposite No 853 was working on the ex-DSER Harcourt Street line when photographed on 10th April 1950 at Bray. The diagram shows a luggage boot at the far end but this at some time had been incorporated into the First class, possibly as a half-compartment, while the original First class entrance had been suppressed. The adjacent Second class with a lavatory (the latter in line with that of First class) had** been upgraded. Third class comprised two and a half semi-open sections with a lavatory that encroached on the van space. A very elegant vehicle, No 853 was one of a class built in 1901 which were given the numbers 851 to 856 in the GSWR list. This vehicle was not withdrawn until 1959. Its clerestory retained its glazing when photographed.

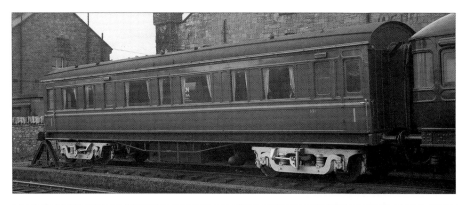

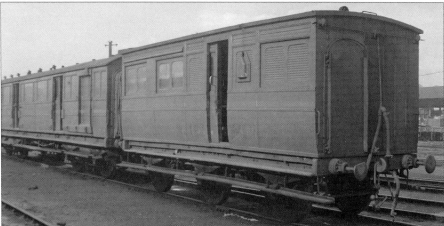

Top left: **Built with a clerestory roof in 1902, No 351 was the principal 'State Carriage' from GSWR days through to the CIE era. Seen at Inchicore on 12th April 1955, it now has modern Commonwealth bogies, making it look like dowager in a mini-skirt. Body dimensions are 50ft by 9ft, it is here coupled to the corridor end of the MGWR Royal Saloon.**

Below left: As **the body of Mail sorting van No 135, which dated from 1877, was only 24ft long, it was always coupled to a larger TPO, in this case No 245 of 1900. Seen at Kingsbridge on 29th October 1951 both TPOs were withdrawn in 1959.**

Below: **This veteran of 1898, Dining car No 343, has become an 'intermediate' car between two of CIE's new 26XX class AEC railcars. Their new carriages just couldn't come fast enough. No 343 was pictured at Inchicore on 8th April 1953.**

Bottom: **Best known of the former WLWR carriages was First class saloon No 900, a 30ft six-wheeler built at Limerick in 1891, part of their 1897 Royal Train. Seen here at Glanmire Road on 20th June 1953, it ended its days as Waterford break-down van No 465A and was eventually preserved at Belturbet.** Charles Friel collection

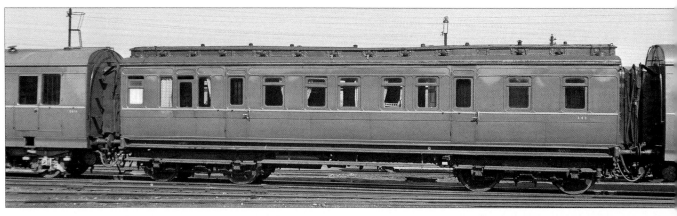

Right: **This rara avis, one of the few WLWR bogies, is Saloon 935, just outshopped at Inchicore on 2nd October 1952. It was built by Metropolitan in 1896 as a vestibuled 48ft Composite. It became an invalid saloon in 1919 and ended its days in 1966 as a mobile studio on the CIE Radio Train.**

Below: **Though 30ft centre van Third No 998 bears evidence of much repanelling by its later owners, it cannot be mistaken for a GSWR vehicle. Built at Limerick by the WLWR in 1895, and seen here at Inchicore in October 1952, it was withdrawn in 1954.**

Right: **WLWR carriages had a distinctive style that set them apart when absorbed into GSWR stock after the takeover. No 937 was a 48ft bogie with a very large van area and only four Third class compartments. Built by Ashbury in 1898, then photographed at Glanmire Road on 16th April 1952, it had lost most of its original panelling. No 937 was withdrawn in 1954.**

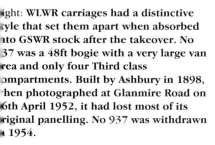

Top: **Stores van No 1055 is seen, awaiting the breakers, at Broadstone on 8th April 1953. It had been converted from a 24ft Third (WLWR No 9, later GSWR No 945) in 1919. It was renumbered 1055 by the GSR who repainted it in their red livery with crest, presumably in the 1930s.**

Above: **Open-platform inspection saloon No 353 of 1912 is shown at Inchicore works on 22nd August 1964. Recently condemned after a minor collision, damage to the platform railings can be seen on the right. It was only 42ft long over headstocks and 9ft wide. No 352 retained its GS&WR livery until around 1950. It had been scheduled to work on** an Irish Railway Record Society special train and its sudden withdrawal was a great disappointment to many members of the society, including the author.

MIDLAND GREAT WESTERN RAILWAY

E L Ahrons was the first writer to describe the Midland as the 'most Irish' of Irish railways, and other visitors have been inclined to agree with him. Its locomotives and carriages were without doubt markedly different in linea-ments to those of its neighbours. Much of this is due to the man who ran that department from 1872 to 1900, and his name was Martin Atock. He was a Lancashire man, one of a fam-ily of railway engineers. Atock believed in reg-ular renewal of engines and carriages and put this into practice on the MGWR, yet many of his engines saw out steam on CIE and his six-wheeled carriages seemed indestructible. The distinctive style of coachbuilding carried out under his command will be evident from the illustrations. His successor, Edward Cusack, initiated a different pattern of panelling with markedly rounded corners that was distinctive in itself without harming the Midland ambi-ence. Cusack also introduced a 'low elliptical' roof contour that could not be mistaken for the GNR version. There were more than 400 coaching vehicles in MGWR stock at the amal-gamation. Second class had been abolished in 1914 and the 24 all Second coaches were divided between the First and Third class lists. Midland numbering was mildly infuriating, but fascinating. The company had retained the tra-ditional practice of numbering each type of vehicle in a separate list, with the inevitable contradictions. The First class coaches num-bered 47, there were 113 Thirds and 41 Com-posites, a State Carriage and three Dining Cars in the same list, but the former was un-num-bered), four Post Office vans (two more were in the Brake van list), 23 carriage trucks, 59 horseboxes, 63 Brake-and luggage vans though several of these had Third class com-partments, and some Composite slip coaches had brake compartments. Two mortuary vans and two Stores vans were also included. The 75 Fish vans had their own list, as had two Per-manent Way department sleeping vans and Tower van No 1. Other service vehicles down-graded from passenger use turned up in the Goods Brake van list along with a purpose-made bogie Locomotive department sleeping van No 47, built in 1909, and a Traffic depart-ment sleeper No 49, six-wheeled and built 1890. Many of the above still existed in the 1950s to provide rich pickings for the carriage-potter.

Atock's programme of complete renewal of passenger stock commenced in 1879. His first standard underframe was timber-built with a 12ft wheelbase, carrying a body 30ft by 9ft with four First class compartments. Next to appear were eight Lavatory-firsts 31ft long with three compartments and a coupé, coming from Ash-bury in 1893/4. Broadstone carriage shops were fully employed into the next century. Atock's Seconds, built from 1880 were 30ft long with four compartments and a central lug-gage boot with double doors. Two of the sev-enteen built had lavatories, not usual in Second class. From 1914, these and three oth-ers were made First class, the remainder becoming Thirds. Renewal of Composite stock began in 1885. In two years 33 were built with the arrangement of Second, First, First, Sec-ond. Two were rebuilt as slip-coaches with one First, two Seconds and a Brake compartment. Third class passengers had to wait till 1890 for new stock, 5-compartment Thirds on 30ft underframes. Two end compartments had a half-partition between them and there was a ladies' compartment at the other end. Produc-tion went into overdrive, 77 of these being built from 1890 to 1900.

Let us now discuss the six-wheeled Saloons, of which there had been four. Composite No 5 was built by Dawson in 1847. Broadstone rebuilt it in 1891 when it lost its middle pair of wheels and gained a clerestory roof. It was now regarded as an Inspection car and became First class No 31 in 1914. Seen in the sidings at Inchicore by the writer in 1944, it was magnif-icent in MGWR lake with gold leaf transfers. Judging from its its remarkable condition it had been under cover for a long time. The maker's plate, still bearing the number 5, read, 'Broadstone 1891'. It is said to have been used by that sporting lady, Empress Elizabeth of Austria, on her equestrian visits to Ireland. This claim has also been made for Dargan's saloon, but somehow the erstwhile No 5 seemed to suit such a personage better; Dargan's saloon is a hulking great thing in comparison but one suspects that Broadstone made a complete renewal of No 5. Unfortunately, when this pretty carriage was seen, there was a ban on photography and to the best of my knowledge no picture of it has survived.

Having mentioned the 'Dargan', now is the time to get it out of the way. It was built, again by Dawson, in 1844 for the Dublin & Drogheda on the instructions of its engineer, Sir John MacNeill. There was an almighty row when the D&D Board found out and refused to take it. William Dargan himself, well-known for his decency, took it off Dawson's hands in 1851, and when he had completed his contract for the Galway line, presented it to the Midland. It was the MGWR State Carriage after that, getting a new underframe and Mansell wheels in 1886. A lavatory was installed in 1904 when it was given the handsome but impractical blue and white livery and numbered 47 in the Compos-ite list. It reverted to brown livery in 1910 and became all-First in 1914, keeping the number 47. The GSR painted it crimson but by the time the 'Dargan' reached the Belfast Transport Museum in 1964 it was again blue. As it approaches its 160th birthday, one can now admire its domed roof and elegantly curved plate glass corner windows in the Railway Gallery of the Ulster Folk and Transport Museum at Cultra.

The two other Family saloons came from Metropolitan Carriage and Wagon in 1879. Their layout was as follows: luggage-boot; retiring rooms (a large compartment with washbasin and small table, plus an adjoining lavatory), saloon and domestics' compart-ment. Later the two, Nos 37 and 38 became all-Firsts. No 38 was destroyed by fire at Athlone in 1942; No 37 was seen consigned to Inchicore for repairs and badly in need of paint, in 1952. Seen again in 1953 at Broad-stone, it had reached the end of its line.

At the very end of his career, Atock aban-doned his conservatism, put a leading bogie under his last design of express locomotive and ordered four bogie Tricomposites from Metropolitan. These were delivered in 1900 and had two compartments for each class, four lavatories (though none for the Thirds) and a luggage boot. The roof profile was low-elliptical though not as pronounced as the later Cusack roof. Numbers were 31, 39, 40 and 41. There was some rearrangement internally over the years. The bodies were 53ft long.

The last passenger six-wheelers were built by Cusack in the early 1900s. Three were four-compartment Firsts, with and without lavato-ries. There was coloured glass in the top-quarterlights and the low-elliptical roof contour looked very smart. It was used also on a Brake-third and several six-wheeled passen-ger vans. Cusack ushered his company into the bogie age with a flourish, the drawing office bringing out designs for two Limited Mail trains. The Lancaster Carriage and Wagon Company were awarded the contract for two First class saloons, two Dining cars and two open Second class bogies. Broadstone built two bogie vans and some experimental Third class bogies. Only the First and Second class coaches were gangwayed at first, and there was electric light, even in the Brake vans, though the Third class still had oil lighting. The length of these vehicles was 54ft. The Limited Mail sets were built in 1902. The dining cars, Nos 1 and 2 in a new series, had clerestory roofs and ran on six-wheeled bogies. In their later years they were to be found on a variety of CIE ser-vices, A pleasant memory is of morning coffee in 1M on a Waterford train, lulled by the chat-ter of twelve wheels over the rail joints. Dining car No 3 came out in 1904; it had a short career as such, but apart from being a twelve wheeler it remains a mystery. Altered to Third class No 108, it swapped bogies with the Royal Saloon (q.v.) and had two saloons and two lavatories. It was burnt along with No 38M at Athlone in 1942. Gangwayed side-corridor stock became the norm after that. Body length was increased to 60ft in 1923 when what were described as the finest Thirds in Ireland were built on Bel-gian underframes. The four Thirds and four Composites built in 1924 were the last coaches to be completed under the old regime, but five more Composites were turned out by the GSR.

The best has been left to the last. The Mid-land contribution to the plethora of Royal trains prepared for Edward VII's post-corona-

Top left: **As mentioned on the previous page, Atock's last carriage design for the Midland was for the four bogie Tricomposites built by the Metropolitan Carriage and Wagon Company in 1900. This is one of the quartet No 31M, seen at Kingsbridge on 29th October 1951, apparently now running as an all Third. Much altered internally from its original configuration, No 31M was withdrawn in 1960.**

Below left: **The value of former MGWR bogie stock to a company with limited resources is demonstrated by the alterations and modifications made during their long careers. This is 94M, seen at Kingsbridge on 20th April 1957 after conversion to an ambulance car. Such vehicles were in demand for pilgrimage traffic. No 94M is barely recognisable as one of the original Lancasters of 1902, but the Cusack roof remains.**

tion tour of Ireland in 1903 was the magnifi cent State Carriage of that year. Generall recognised to have been the apogee of Iris coachbuilding, it has been adequatel described more than once. On a 54ft unde frame and with pressed steel four-whee bogies, the body was 56ft long, bow-ended an with domed roof. At one end, a small observa tion section, also referred to as a smokin saloon, gave on to the main saloon. Th entrance hall and adjacent lavatory was on th central axis, and beyond these was the dinin saloon served by a small galley with gangwaye access to carriages for courtiers and officer. The interior was panelled by the Dublin firm Millar and Beatty in a sumptuous classical styl with splendidly carved Corinthian column. The State Carriage retained its blue and whit livery until repainted in MGWR lake in Jun 1924. Transferred to Inchicore, where it she tered in the carriage paint shop and wa painted GSR red, retaining the MGW coat-o arms, its last outing was probably in th Eucharistic Congress year of 1932 when it wa marshalled with its GSWR equivalent in a trai carrying the Papal Legate, the Pope's rovin ambassador. Unexpectedly, it was seen in 195 painted CIE green and bearing the number 34 (allocated by the GSR in 1925) for the fir time. There was always the hope that it was to good to scrap, and it transcended any politic. animus, or so we thought. On a visit t Inchicore Works in 1964 one's worst fea were realised. The Royal was out of doors, ha ing been made a temporary office for som time-and-motion boffins. And it was unlocke The interior was ankle-deep in discarded com puter software and Millar and Beatty's hand work had been vandalised. Those delica Corinthian columns were lying round like s many skittles. What a sad end to Irish craft manship.

Above: **The apogee of Irish craftsmanship, the Midland State Carriage of 1903 as latterly painted in CIE green and at last carrying the number 346, allocated (in the GS&WR list) by GSR in 1925. The previous livery had been a vaguely reddish-brown, possibly what remained of the 'dark lake'** applied in 1924. Pictured against the mock mediaeval splendour of Inchicore Works on 12th April 1955, the State Carriage suits those six-wheel bogies very well. They had previously been under MGWR Dining car No 3, change had been made in 1915.

Above: **The corridor end of the State Carriage was not often photographed. This useful view taken on 27th April 1957 shows how well it was arranged. No 346 had been turned, and is standing on the main line at Inchicore with the Ballyfermot housing estate in the background and is coupled to a new aluminium brake van. One wonders what went on that day.** N Simmons, courtesy M Davies

Centre Right: **Post Office Sorting Van 2M seen at Boston sidings on 12th April 1952, was one of a class of four built in 1887/8 at Broadstone.**

Bottom: **No 163M, a 54ft corridor composite bogie, is seen fresh out of the paint shop in the short lived GSR brown and cream livery. Built at Broadstone during Cusack's regime in 1903 as First-Second composite No 44, it had been converted to an all First when Second class was abolished. Its configuration has been changed again, in this view it is a First-third composite. It was later converted to an ambulance coach.** C Casserley

Left: **Still in good shape, a post-war MGWR side-corridor Composite forms part of a mixed train at Ballinrobe on 23rd June 1959. This was one of four such 9ft 6in wide coaches built at Broadstone in 1924 on 60ft Belgian underframes. Five more were completed by the GSR. One of the leading authorities on Ireland's railways, the late Bob Clements, considered the Midland bogie Thirds of that period to be the finest in Ireland.**

Centre: **Stores van numbered 63M in the Van list and photographed on 27th March 1951, lingered around Inchicore yard for many years. It had an interesting previous existence as a combined TPO and Brake van. Four of these, numbered 24-27, were built by Brown, Marshall & Co in 1885 to Atock's 30ft standard length. Nos 25 and 27 were replaced by similar vehicles (but with 'Cusack' roofs) in 1908/9. One of these became the Stores Van. The remaining pair continued as Postal vehicles until 1924 when their nets were removed,. They remained in use as ordinary vans until CIE days.**

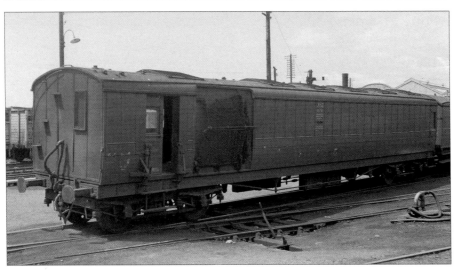

Left and opposite page top: **The six-wheel TPO No 1 was destroyed in the Civil War and a replacement was put in hand at Broadstone. At 60ft long, it was the largest TPO in Ireland, though it was not completed until 1925 after the formation of the GSR who numbered it, 1M. Both sides are illustrated to show that it could exchange mailbags in either direction without being turned. These pictures of 1M were taken shortly before it left Galway on an up express on 11th June 1957. The adjacent vehicle is a six-wheel Brake van, 21D.**

Above: **This horsebox with a hounds' compartment, found at the Broadstone on 8th April 1953, is No 60M. It looks much older than its building date of 1901.**

Right: **Carriage truck 10M of 1921, seen at Kingsbridge goods station on 19th April 1954, was clearly due for a visit to the paint shop.**

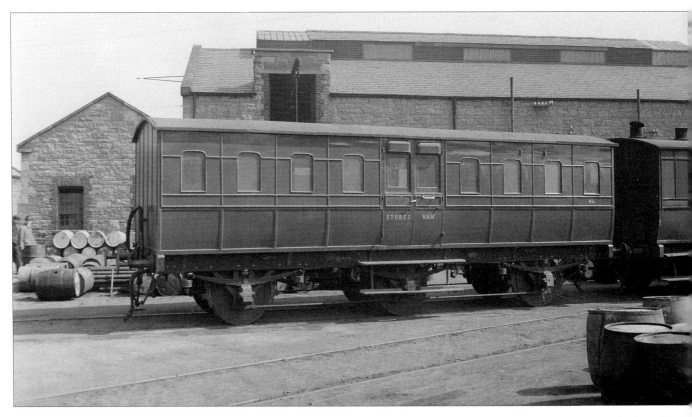

Above: **Stores van 41M built at Broadstone in 1883 but found use at Inchicore when the MGWR works closed.**

Below: **Another Inchicore Stores van, with the Departmental number 306A, is seen there on 3rd October 1955. Another Broadstone product, its unusual unequal double doors, and its asymmetrical panelling implies a conversion from** another class of coaching vehicle. A third Inchicore stores van was another ex-MGWR six-wheeler No 63M, seen on page 22.

Above: **A purpose-built bogie sleeping van for enginemen must have been meant as a kindly act, but drivers on lodging turns would tell you they avoided it like the plague and would sooner spend a night on their footplate. Built in 1909, No 108A,** its MGWR number was 47, was reputedly infested with bed-bugs! It is seen here at Westport on 23rd June 1959.

Below: **Another Midland oddity was 70M, the centre-van six-wheeler that spent its** last days on the Inchicore workmens' train. By 2nd October 1952, it had been repainted in Departmental grey and numbered 300A. It is a curious hybrid with a Cusack roof and Atock panelling, it is believed to be a rebuild of 1910.

DUBLIN & SOUTH EASTERN RAILWAY

Here was another railway that persisted with the practice of having separate lists for each class and type. The GSR made things worse for inquisitive enthusiasts by half-heartedly renumbering some in a 2XX series. Perhaps it would have been better to re-number the stock from scratch in 1925. Around 250 passenger vehicles (of which some 40 were Brake vans) were in the lists at amalgamation. The situation regarding 'other coaching vehicles' is less clear. The 21 horseboxes had their own list, while carriage trucks and fish vans, both in the former category, had low numbers in the goods register. The passenger vans were numbered 1 to 47, but the series included some 'cattle brakes' (the equivalent of 'drovers' brakes on other lines) and two Post Office vans.

Second class had been eliminated from 1st January 1922. The 17 carriages destroyed in the Civil War included some of the company's best stock; many more were damaged to a greater or lesser extent, and as there were other vehicles with other infirmities the DSER stock totals were drastically reduced. The few bogie carriages inherited by the GSR (33 at a rough estimate) were consequently looked after somewhat better than the legion of six-wheelers, though the more recent of these were still found on Dublin suburban services in CIE days.

The DWWR had not made intensive use of the carriage shop at Grand Canal Street at first, going across the water for new construction. Among carriage suppliers used in the nineteenth century were Ashbury, Brown Marshall and the Birmingham Carriage and Wagon Co. The last indigenous firm to supply coaching stock to the DWWR was Martin of North Wall who built 4-wheel Passenger brakes from 1878

to 1881. The most energetic locomotive superintendent was Richard Cronin (1897-1917) who introduced larger six-wheelers with the distinctive parabolic roof contour and a series of three-coach bogie sets for the Westland Row-Bray service, all hauled by a modern (for the time) fleet of suburban tank engines. They were still going strong in the 1950s. The first two bogie carriages were Tricomposites built by Birmingham Carriage and Wagon the year before Cronin took the reins. One went in the Troubles; the other lasted to be seen as Lavatory-third No 203D in the 1950s. They were 44ft long. The last DSER bogies, for local use, were 58ft over body. Of superior carriages, the line's solitary clerestory was noteworthy, forming part of an inaugural restaurant car train in 1904 on the new route to Waterford via Macmine Junction, in opposition to the GSWR. A gangwayed bogie Brake van was converted to Kitchen car, serving First and Second class saloons. Later a bogie Third was added, making an Irish 'first' for serving meals to all three classes. A Composite diner with central kitchen was built in 1905 and used with another pair of modified coaches. All these were turned out by the little Grand Canal Street factory, along with a Directors' saloon in 1907. The Midland's 'Royal' was occasionally borrowed when visiting VIPs disembarked at Kingstown Pier. It is almost obligatory to mention the early history of two other bogie vehicles. The first decade of the last century saw a great craze for steam railmotors to answer the threat posed by urban electric tramways. These had been the bane of the DWWR since 1896. Thus, the company went to Manning Wardle of Leeds for two railmotors. Being engine-builders, Manning Wardle sub-contracted the coach bodies to the Brush Electrical Engineering Company. Delivered in 1906, the railcars did precisely the opposite of what was expected of them - they drove intending passengers on to the trams. It was all due to the appaling vibration generated by the power units. Steam railmotors as a whole were prone to vibration, but the DWWR cars must have

been the worst of the lot. In less than two years the cars had their motive power removed and they were converted to ordinary Tricomposite carriages. Later altered to Thirds, in this form they remained on their home territory for many years numbered 209D and 212D.

Of the 21 horseboxes that passed to the GSR, 13 were built at intervals from 1896 to the company's standard design, one had been acquired second-hand from the Finn Valley Railway and six were of an 1879 Ashbury design. No 21 had been built on a 30ft six-wheeled passenger underframe to the order of a rich racing enthusiast and was bought back for £40 when he apparently tired of it. No other 6-wheeled horseboxes, apart from the two built by the BCDR in 1890, are known to have run in Ireland. No 21 was scrapped in 1928. There was a '200' series of odds-and-ends of which the best known was 200D itself, frequently found hanging around Westland Row). This was the inevitable mortuary van, a four-wheeler later converted for fish traffic, with two pairs of double doors on either side.

This page, bottom:

A five compartment six-wheel First, 15D, has Cronin's high parabolic roof contour and the 34ft 6in body length of the period. It was built at Grand Canal Street 'factory' in 1906 and looks in good condition at Westland Row on 12th April 1952. It was withdrawn in 1959.

Opposite page:

Top: **Lavatory-third 203D had started life as Dublin, Wicklow & Wexford Railway's Composite No 12, built by Birmingham Carriage & Wagon in 1895 as one of the company's first bogie carriages. It stands in evening sunshine at Harcourt Street terminus on 29th October 1951.**

Centre: **This semi-open gangwayed bogie First was the only clerestory coach owned by the DSER and fortunately survived many vicissitudes to become 12D on the GSR and CIE, even though much altered. Built as one of the DWWR's first restaurant cars at Grand Canal Street in 1903, it is seen outside Inchicore carriage shops on 18th April 1952.**

Bottom: **The DSER had two TPO vans, both six-wheelers, at the time of the GSR takeover. Numbered 32 and 33, they were built at Grand Canal Street in 1893 and survived until 1958. No 33D is show in Kingsbridge sidings on 19th April 1954, newly painted in plain green with bilingual instructions for the Late Fee letter box in gold. These vehicles were only 28ft long and weighed 12 tons.**

Below and centre: **The sad tale of the DSER railmotors has been referred to earlier on page 26. On 10th April 1950, open Third 209D, the former railmotor No 1 is hale and hearty in a local train at Bray, while its fellow 212D was decaying on the Inchicore Dump. Comparison with the** lower photograph of No 2 in its original condition shows how removal of the engine resulted in the asymmetrical wheelbase and also the carriage solebars overlapping the engine cab. Four windows across the 'driving' end of the coach body were retained when the Guard's compartment was made Third class. The railmotors were Tricompos and numbered 19 and 20 on removal of the engine units, becoming Third class in 1930/31. Incidentally No 2 had Marshall's valve gear whereas its companion had Walschaerts gear.
Courtesy, The Green Studio

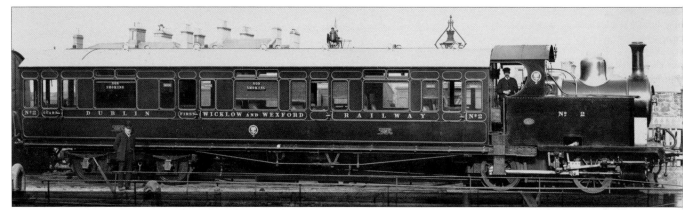

This is an example of the standard DSER horsebox turned out by the Factory. No 8D which dated from 1913 and lasted until 1961 was seen at Kingsbridge Goods on 29th October 1951.

Horsebox 14D was the last of its kind to survive when photographed at Waterford Manor station on 21st April 1954. It was an Ashbury vehicle of 1879 and had replaced the W&TR's Dawson horsebox when the GSR took control in 1925.

Above: There was not much scope for originality in carriage truck design but companies did aspire to their own 'house style'. The DSER achieved individuality by numbering these particular vehicles in the wagon list. Such a vehicle, No 194D is awaiting attention at Broadstone wagon works on 23rd April 1954.

Below: The rather modest DSER carriage truck is dwarfed by this vehicle, CIE No 1045, photographed at Kingsbridge on 20th April 1957. This is one of two ex-Waterford & Limerick carriage trucks built at Limerick in 1887. These were the only six-wheel open carriage trucks to run in Ireland. They were adapted for milk traffic in 1948 and lasted until 1961.

THE RAILWAYS OF COUNTY CORK

Whether or not it was a result of the city's topography, every railway company of the six whose lines terminated in Cork insisted on having its own station. Five of the six were broad gauge concerns, one of which (the Cork Blackrock & Passage) might have refrained from converting to narrow gauge had an early decision been taken to meet and exchange traffic. It took an English company to provide capital for the Cork City Railways to cross the two arms of the River Lee and connect, in 1912, with the first railway into the city, though to mix metaphors, this is all water under the bridge. The latter railway, the Cork & Bandon, opened its Albert Quay terminus on 6 December 1851. The 'Bandon' spread its tentacles over west Cork to link the city with principal towns and seaports though they were all sadly depopulated since the Hungry Forties), changing its name to Cork Bandon & South Coast in 1888. A route mileage of 96 and a coaching stock total of 68 serve to emphasise the scarcity of business, but the CBSC was a fascinating line and sadly neglected by railway devotees, partly due to its comparative isolation.

The CBSC abolished Second class travel from 1st May 1907, after which date passenger carriages, including Brake vans, were numbered somewhat chaotically in a single series from 1 to 76. There were 17 blanks in the list and 59 carriages would have passed to the GSR in 1925 had not five of these been lost in 1923, the year in which the burning of coaching stock became almost a national sport. The most interesting coaches were bogie vehicles of several different lengths that varied from 33ft to 49ft over body. Eight of the shorter variety

were built between 1890 and 1899 for through excursion trains from Cork to the seaside village of Courtmacaherry via the T&CELR. There were 33ft Third class bogies with six compartments and 34ft Firsts with five, as well as a First class saloon and two 33ft bogie Brake vans. These reminded one of the short bogie coaches in 'O' gauge built by Messrs Bing in the early 1900s. Further bogie stock for main line use was built between 1905 and 1914, in which year the quantity of eight-wheelers on the CBSC had risen to a creditable 45% of the total. The later ones included Lavatory-composites. Vintage specimens that survived included 5-compartment six-wheelers taken over with the West Cork Railway in 1880. In the early 1900s, eight of the original DNGR coaches of the 1870s were bought. Typical Wolverton products, some lasted into CIE days. The remaining CBSC coaching stock included 4 horseboxes, 2 carriage trucks and 3 fish vans.

The nine mile long branch from Ballinascarthy on the CBSC Clonakilty branch to Courtmacsherry was a baronially-guaranteed affair belonging to two companies, the Ballinascarthy & Timoleague Light Rly, and the T&CELR. The latter, seemingly the operating company, had a winding roadside line following the Argadeen River through charming scenery to Courtmacsherry. The T&C had four passenger carriages, a bogie Third and a Composite, both 23ft long and dating from 1889, and two others built in 1892 by the Bristol Wagon Co. These were 30-footers, a Brake-composite and a Brake-third. The seasonal excursions kept the branch open until 1960, but the entire west Cork system closed completely in 1961.

Cork & Macroom Direct Railway

Macroom, in the valley of the River Lee, was served from May 1866 by the Cork & Macroom Direct Railway, which entered the city by a junction with the Bandon line a mile short of

the latter company's terminus at Albert Quay. This being Cork, the arrangement lasted only until 1879, when the CMDR opened its own terminus at Capwell. The GSR lost no time in reinstating Macroom Junction and closed Capwell in 1925. The once-profitable CMDR, 25 miles long, lost its passenger trains in 1931 and freight services in 1953. Like the GSWR, the Macroom company still offered Second class accommodation in 1925 but in the CMDR's case this was promptly withdrawn by the GSR. At the Irish 'grouping' the CMDR possessed 33 coaching vehicles, including a number of original four and six-wheelers built in 1865 by the Ashbury Railway Carriage and Iron Company of Manchester. One of the Ashburys, No 1R, was photographed in 1948 as a four-compartment six-wheel Third class with a 28ft long body. It had been downgraded from First class ten years before. This had an unusual body style with glazed top-quarters, a very deep waist panel and a circular inset panel on each door for the class designation. It had retained ancient features like spoked wheels and oil-pot lamp tops, the latter converted to acetylene gas lighting. While the old Irish manufacturers had been put out of business by the 'in-house' activities of the larger railways, an interesting enterprise appeared on the scene. The South of Ireland Wagon Company was established at Cappoquin on the Waterford, Dungarvan & Lismore line, probably during 1878 when the latter railway opened. A Macroom carriage that survived as Cork breakdown van No 128A has been identified as a product of the Cappoquin company. It was severely wagon-like in construction, a four-wheeled five-compartment Third class with a straight-sided body 24ft long and outside framing. The CMDR took advantage of bargains offered by the GSWR when it absorbed the WDLR and others in 1900, obtaining several WDLR carriages, some of which may have been built at Cappoquin though records are sketchy. More 'coach-like' passenger stock on the WDLR had distinctive styling with vertical mouldings below the waist. One example was 16R, photographed in 1951. It was a straight-sided four-wheel five-compartment Third with 26ft body, reputedly built by the Metropolitan Co. in 1876. Perhaps most fascinating of a very mixed bag was a Cork Blackrock & Passage six-wheel first saloon that became CMDR No 4. New construction ordered between 1893 and 1900 included three five-compartment Seconds and a Brake-third from the Birmingham Railway Carriage and Wagon Company and four five-compartment Thirds from Ashbury. The CMDR took a leaf out of the Bandon's book in 1896 by acquiring two bogie Thirds from the Lancaster Company. These were 36ft 6in long with seven compartments, while the CBSC's Thirds were 33ft, with six compartments. The Macroom's last purchase came in 1921. CMDR Nos. 7 and 8 had been GNR six-wheelers built in the 1880s, an R5 Composite and U2 Third respectively.

Opposite page: **A CBSCR train at Cork Albert Quay in an undated view, but which, judging from the cleanliness of the engine and stock, was probably taken before World War One. The leading coach has six compartments and, from the break in the lower footboards, is one of the line's short bogie Thirds.**
Courtesy, H Richards

Above: **This wonderful museum piece had served under three owners by the time it was removed from the main Irish railway network and placed on the entirely detached rails of the Waterford & Tramore line. Only the vacuum brake gear and livery of the fourth owner dispel the atmosphere of complete antiquity. No 24B had been built for the West Cork Railway in 1865 and was approaching its ninetieth birthday when the W&T section was dieselised. It was recorded at Tramore on 21st April 1954.**

Centre: **Bandon carriage truck No 4B looks well in CIE green livery, when seen at Albert Quay on 20th August 1954. The large diameter, split-spoke carriage wheels are noticeable when compared with those on the wagon to its left.**

Bottom: **This short First class bogie No 43B, seen at Albert Quay on 15th April 1952, crammed five compartments into a 34ft body which was rather smaller than six-wheelers on the BCDR and the DSER. Painted in a darker shade of green and embellished with two CIE symbols, this may have been done locally.**

Top: **No 10A, seen here in GSR livery was withdrawn in 1949. This Macroom bogie managed to squeeze seven Third class compartments into a 36ft long body.**
Courtesy, The Green Studio

Above: **Two five-compartment Thirds with 29ft bodies built in 1893 by the Birmingham Carriage & Wagon Company, were almost modern by Macroom standards. No 5R, was moved to the Waterford & Tramore section, where it is** **seen in April 1954. The introduction of diesel railcars in 1955 meant there was only one summer left for steam traction and coaching stock like this, on the W&T.**

WATERFORD & TRAMORE RAILWAY

A seven-mile long broad gauge railway that kept its independence for 72 years and its isolation until closure in 1960, the W&T remained as it were, in a surreal time-warp and virtually unaltered until becoming part of the GSR in 1925. William Dargan, who built the line, literally set things in motion by agreeing to provide engines and rolling stock for a matter of months. Services began in September 1853, and some of Dargan's carriages may well have been retained by the W&T, as was the venerable single-driver of the 1830s that was kept lovingly until 1912. Fifteen carriages and a Brake van appear in the 1867 census and it is worth mentioning that none of the former (with a possible exception mentioned later) had brakes, nor were automatic continuous brakes fitted after the 1889 Regulation Act. The loophole found by the W&T was a clause that required trains entering a terminus to be under the control of the Guard's handbrake. There were no intermediate stopping places on the W&T. Harold Fayle, pioneer historian and photographer of Irish railways, was born in Clonmel and became a frequent visitor to

Tramore in his boyhood. It is easy to find flaws in Fayle's writing but he recorded many intimate details of the line - and its equipment. A list of coaching stock prepared by the W&T in 1924, provided a starting point for evaluation by the late Bob Clements in 1957. His comments are soundly based, and the list as expanded by these is given below.

When describing the Tramore carriages, it is worth remembering that both termini had a single platform on the west or up side of the line. This abolished the need for doors on the off-side, or if they had been delivered with their full quota, those on the east side were permanently locked and the handles removed. First class No 1 was photographed by Henry Casserley in June 1932 and by great good fortune views from either end were recorded. That of the 'coupé' end has been seen before and has misled some people into assuming that what Hamilton Ellis termed the 'chariot end' was the 'boot' that concealed the folding bed. Unfortunately it takes the full length of a First class compartment to provide space for recumbent human beings, and the writer, looking at what seems to be another coupé at the far end, dismissed the story as myth. That is, until Richard Casserley produced his father's second picture. This agrees in general with Head's description (see page 7) of the MGWR carriage. Head was no doubt correct in

describing this compartment as a coupé, there being only one row of seats, facing an end window. Opposite these would be the 'table' or shelf concealing the folding beds, though in No 1's case probably one bed, as the single end window would not permit the central partition he described. But look at the curved-glass corner windows and marvel at their survival over most of a century. Further study of both images shows that the interior has been altered. Two partitions have been removed, dividing the coach into two saloons and these are joined by a glazed door. No 1 seems to have been used as a 'club car' to take local nabobs to and from Tramore races. But it must have arrived on the W&T complete with bed, which would have gone when the alterations were made. Fayle refers only to a 'tradition' about the bed. Clements thought that Dawson had built this carriage for the MGWR in 1847. No 2 looked to be contemporary; it is to the left of No 1 in the view taken under the roof at Waterford Manor station which appears on page 9.

Nos 4, 9 and 10, (ex WDLR) were alike except for their wheels. The vertical mouldings below the waist were uncommon. The W&T had asked Dawsons that the 'opens' (First No 6 and Thirds Nos 5 and 6) should be similar to the 'Kingstown' coaches, showing that the latter were more popular than one would have thought. But they were soon glazed on the offside. The open First had five compartments. Confusingly, when Third class No 6 third was withdrawn by the GSR, the former took its place as No 6W. The original open Third had six compartments. Third No 5 differed from either of the others. A distant view shows it to have had six normal divisions with a narrow one at the end, probably for a brakesman. First class Nos 7 and 8 were replacements ordered from Metropolitan. Both had five compartments but curiously, differed in length by one foot. No 7 was externally severe in outline and had outside axleguards as favoured by some northern lines. But compartments were uncomfortably narrow for First class; 5ft 6in at most, exclusive of cushioning.

The more conventional Thirds were camera-shy. Nos 1 and 2 may have been original Dawson Firsts downgraded. No 3, coming from Metropolitan a year after Firsts Nos 7 and 8, had compartments scarcely more than 5ft long passengers perched on 18in shelves. Reverting to the open-sided Thirds, the difference in length was no more than 1ft 5in and a brake wheel, if any, would have overlapped the end. This practice was not unknown. No 9 was a former Dawson First of 1853, complete with dog-box. It was erroneously described as an Ashbury by Fayle and Newham in their 1964 publication on the W&T. Grouping Third-brakes into a separate series may have occurred on arrival of the Pickering two-compartment carriage in 1913. Amusingly, the makers fitted No 1 with a vacuum brake, probably as a matter of course. Nos 2 and 3 of the brake-ended series must be sought for with a magnifying glass in views of W&T trains.

FIRST CLASS

No.	Wheels	Length	Builder	Compartments/Description	Withdrawn
1	6	27ft 6in	Dawson 1853*	'Bed Carriage' 4 (see text)	1933
2	6	24ft	Dawson 1853	4	1933
3	6	27ft 3in		second hand replacement (1892) 5	1933
4	6	26ft	MC&W 1878	for WDLR, ex GSWR 4	1933
5	6	27ft 6in	Ashbury 1877	(replacement) 5	1941
6	6	26ft 10in	Dawson 1857	(to Third class 1936) Open, 5,	1941
7	6	27ft 6in	MC&W 1891	(replacement)(to Third class 1936) 5	1937
8	6	28ft 6in		other details as for No 7, above	1937
9	4	26ft	MC&W	ex GSWR 1900 4	1941
10	4	26ft		other details as for No 9 above 4	1941

Nos 1 and 2 were probably built earlier

THIRD CLASS

No.	Wheels	Length	Builder / Description	Withdrawn
1	6	24ft	listed as 1894 possibly ex- First class from then 5	1933
2	6	24ft	listed as 1895 possibly ex- First class from then 4	1937
3	4?	26ft 3in	MC&W 1892 as 3rd 5	1937
4	4	26ft	Dawson 1857 (replaced by No 6 ex- First) Open, 6	1937?
5	6	25ft	listed as 1900 ex-GSWR ,ex-W&CI	1933
6	6	24ft 7in	Dawson 1857 Open, 6	1937
			not in the 1924 list, believed to be the original No 2 Third brake	
			not in the 1924 list, believed to be the original No 3 Third brake	
9	6	26ft 6in	listed as 1900 probably. ex First Dawson 1853, 6	1937
10	6	26ft	probably ex-GSWR(WDL)1900 5	1937 (/9/3?)

THIRD BRAKE (renumbering a late 1913 decision)

No.	Wheels	Length	Builder	Compartments/Description	Withdrawn
1	6	?	Pickering 1913	2 plus brake	1946
2	6	24ft	very old	2 plus brake	1941
3	6	26ft 9in	very old	2 plus brake	1941

Fayle writes of a W&T horsebox, not mentioned in the 1924 list. The GSR drafted in an 1879 Ashbury box from the DSER. It suited the timeless atmosphere of the Manor terminus splendidly. Again, thanks to Fayle, we can describe the carriage liveries of the W&T: First class was dark blue, lined in white whilst Third class was reddish brown lined in black. Block capital transfers, yellow blocked with red, were used for class lettering. Carriage numbers appeared in a garter transfer bearing the company's title though this was not always used. Many vehicles retained the old W&T livery to the last and Fayle also mentions several ordinary carriages having end windows. This is borne out by photographs, though no set pattern can be established.

Above: **Before the GSR imprint was laid on the Waterford & Tramore, somebody arranged to have the Fairbairn single No 2 pose in Waterford yard with three of the original First class carriages. The 'open'** **First No 6, glazed and doorless on the offside, leads its two Dawson built companions, 4-compartment No 2 and the chariot ended No 1.**

Below: **Third class open No 6, in the process of being dismantled on 11th June 1932, had not been repainted since acquisition by the GSR in 1925.**
H C Casserley.

Right and centre right: **Two views of saloon No 1 are needed to appreciate the subtlety of Dawson's design. Recorded on 11th June 1932, the left-hand end, with curved corners, does at least show that this compartment had length enough for a folding bed, though it was not the vehicle that Sir Francis Head had seen on the MGWR - there would have been a longitudinal partition dividing the end window in two. It can also be seen that the interior has been altered to make one large saloon. The carved 'chariot' end to the coupe' is another pleasant touch. The acetylene gas producer comes as a surprise, but is an antiquity in itself.** H C Casserley.

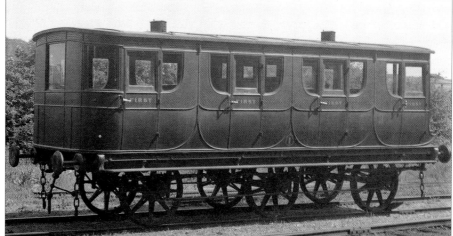

Below: **The Midland Carriage & Wagon Company built this five-compartment First, seen here as GSR No 7W in July 1934, as a replacement in 1891. The compartments are uncommonly narrow for First class, perhaps the W&T reckoned that as the line was a mere seven miles long, they would be tolerable enough. There appear to be windows in both ends.** H C Casserley

GREAT SOUTHERN
RAILWAYS

By 1915 the GSWR had used most of the consecutive numbers from 1 to 1139 for its coaching stock and decided that future construction should be numbered in blocks according to class and type: from 140 onwards for First class, 1290 for Thirds, 1890 for Third class and brakes, 2090 for Composites, 2540 for Brake and parcels vans, 2950 for Post Office sorting vans and 2980 onwards for horseboxes. Here they almost caught up with a series, Nos 3046-3065, that had been allocated to four-wheeled refrigerator vans in 1901. The GSR followed the same practice, continuing Inchicore's post-war building programme to established GSWR designs, elliptical-roofed coaches with timber bodies on 57ft steel underframes, exclusively side-corridor at first. In 1931 the last of the traditional main line coaches to be built were a pair of Dining cars, Nos 2400 and 2401. They were designed to run as a unit; 2400 had a central kitchen between two saloons, 2401 being solely a dining saloon. They were mounted on 60ft steel underframes and had a long career on CIE, with many modifications. A series of non-gangwayed suburban coaches was built from 1926 to 1931 on the new standard 60ft underframes and a fleet of 26 horseboxes to a new design, 19ft 6in long by 8ft 2in wide, had been turned out from 1924 to 1927.

There were experiments with new things. Ten steam railcars, four from Sentinel and six from Claytons that carried their fuel and water in a 'boot' at one end were purchased between 1926 and 1928. Tried out on selected branch lines and local services, none of them apparently lived up to expectations, though the Claytons found their eventual niche later as twin-articulated carriages on the Tramore line. Two broad-gauge Drewry cars were no more successful (two on the 3-foot gauge were even worse). Against a background of diesel railcar development that, however limited, was giving the Great Northern some breathing space, it was a pity to see capital wasted. The Drumm battery trains introduced by the GSR in the thirties appeared to have great promise and were invaluable when the wartime fuel shortage began to bite. The Free State government had sponsored Drumm's invention while the GSR provided space at Inchicore for a company to manufacture the alkaline batteries. The GSR built four twin-articulated electric railcar sets, the last two sets being to the new steel-panelled outline, that were capable of multiple-unit working. Whatever the economics involved, the Drumm railcars just faded away when CIE was formed. Weight has always been a drawback with battery propulsion. A Drumm set carried over 13 tons of accumulators, which was the equivalent to dragging a loaded coal wagon behind it.

Going back to 1926, in that year four Pullman cars, the only ones to operate in Ireland, went into service between Dublin, Cork and Limerick. Numbered 100-103 in the Pullman series, they were typical of their era with all the features found on their British equivalents including the umber brown and cream livery. On the conclusion of a ten-year agreement the cars were bought by the GSR.

However gloomy the overall situation was, traffic on the Dublin to Cork line was booming in the 1930s and a radical change in main line carriage design was needed. It was the time of steel-panelled coaches with compartments that had large windows and were entered from the side corridor. External access was via end or centre vestibules only and decor was unfussy. The new concept was embraced wholeheartedly by the Inchicore drawing office. In 1935 the works turned out twelve steel-panelled coaches 60ft long and 9ft wide; one was a seven-compartment First with a lavatory amidships, a design not repeated. There were eight Third class side-corridors with seven compartments and end and centre-vestibules, the latter having a lavatory at either side. There was no intention of slavishly copying Mr Stanier's new Irish Mail that awaited you at Holyhead. Two Composites were arranged thus: vestibule, three First class compartments, First and Third class lavatorys, four Third class compartments and vestibule. The twelfth vehicle was a matching bogie Brake van 60ft long with central Guard's compartment. No more of these were built. From the above, a new Day Mail set was assembled, incorporating three out of four older vehicles refurbished and flush-panelled in steel to match the new ones. They were Diners 2400/2401 and TPOs Nos 2950/1 (GSWR 1919), one of the latter being spare. A further eight main line coaches (four each of Thirds and Composites) were built in 1937. On this occasion, bodies were widened from 9ft to 9ft 6in at waist with a reduction to 9ft at the eaves, giving a 'tumble-home' in both directions.

The long-suffering Dublin commuter had been given a degree of luxury in the previous year when Inchicore produced twelve coaches of three types, Third brakes, Thirds and Composites. The Thirds were open, with a central gangway and strap-hanging facilities. First class sections in the Composites had side corridors. The new suburban stock was intended to run as two six-coach sets but were soon distributed among older stock owing to over-crowding. One novelty was the fan-assisted ventilation in the roof, instead of the familiar Laycock torpedoes.

Excluding the experimental railcars, the GSR had built or acquired 104 coaching vehicles, mostly bogie stock, before Europe was again engulfed in the war that would halt the supply of materials for railway operation and maintenance. The swan-song of the GSR was the construction of the three great locomotives of the 800 class (1939/40) that were fitting motive power for the modern rolling stock.

The GSWR carriage livery was adopted almost in its entirety in 1925. For the first five years the style of serif lettering and numerals remained unaltered. Two small alterations were made to the former company's heraldic device by the GSR, the arms of Kilkenny that had appeared in the top left quarter being replaced by those of Galway and the new company's title appeared on the surrounding garter. The use of the GSR transfer was quite widespread among bogie and rigid-axle carriages. The purple-lake livery (sometimes described as purple-brown) was discontinued in 1930 and replaced by brown below the bottom waist moulding and cream above, not unlike that on the English Great Western Railway's carriages. Six-wheelers and more menial vehicles were given all-over brown. Perhaps this livery was inspired by the appearance of the Pullmans at around this time. This livery had a short life and few photographs show complete trains in the two-colour scheme. One doubts if all the stock achieved brown paint before it was superseded by crimson lake in the mid-1930s. The coat-of-arms continued to be used, almost indiscriminately. However class designations on carriage doors were now applied using florid numbers 1 and 3, very similar to those on the LMS. On carriages of uniform class the number of these figures was reduced, not necessarily appearing on doors themselves. As the 'Emergency' lingered on carriage painting became severely curtailed and many coaches were in quite a disreputable state when CIE was formed in 1945. It has been stated that the four Pullmans purchased from that company in 1936 retained their umber and-cream livery until painted green by CIE. But there must have been some touching-up to obliterate the old name and the Pullman armorial device that appeared twice on each side of the cars. The numbers 100-103 were retained, though these numbers were also carried by four six-wheeled Third brakes, though it is unlikely that anyone would confuse the two types of stock which carried the same designations.

Opposite page, bottom:

One of a dozen steel-panelled non-gangway coaches built for Dublin suburban services in 1936, open Third 1332 catered for 'standees' by having leather straps suspended from rails the length of each open section. These swayed hypnotically in unison when not ballasted by commuters. Note the horizontal fan-operated roof ventilators that revolved effortlessly on ball-bearings. The Green Studio.

Top right: **The corridor side of 8-compartment Lavatory-third No 1317 built in 1925 with external doors to all compartments. The design dated back to 1915. No 1317 is seen at Wexford North on 26th May 1958, with the short-lived Second class designation.**

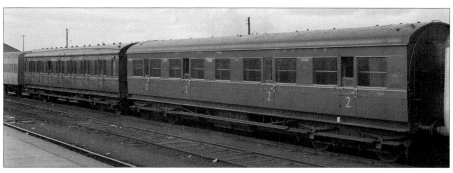

Centre right: **The four Irish Pullmans were built by the Birmingham Railway Carriage & Wagon Co and each seated 46 passengers in two saloons, with tip-up seats in red and black figured moquette (by the 1950s they were not particularly comfortable). The kitchen/pantry was at one end while a lavatory and cupboard that contained wrecking tools was at the other. Internal decor was to Pullman standards though Pullman gangways were not used owing to the need for access from ordinary coaches. Dimensions were: length over headstocks 62ft 4in, over buffers 66ft 1½in; bogie centres 43ft 4in; bogie wheelbase 10ft. The 5ft 3in gauge bogies were reputed to have been built to Pullman design by the LMS. The length over vestibule end body was 63ft 10in. The length over body corner pillars was 57ft 1¾in and the width over mouldings was 8ft 11in. The underframes were Pullman standard steel frames with angle trusses. One of the Pullmans is seen here in its original umber and cream Pullman livery at Kingsbridge.**
Courtesy, Lens of Sutton Association.

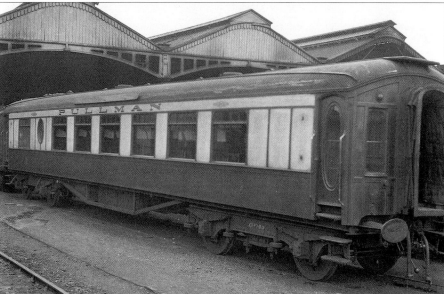

Right: **Bogie Brake van No 2548 was built in 1935 for Bredin's Cork Day Mail set but remained the only one of its kind. It is seen here at Kingsbridge on 20th April 1957.**

Top: **Twin-articulated coaches made their appearance on the GSR when the failed Clayton steam railcars had their motive power excised and re-emerged from Inchicore in three 'pairs'. They were sent to the W&T section; some are seen there on 7th July 1934 in the brown and cream colours of that time. The nearest car is all-** **First, which seems extravagant, but we surmise that the GSR had Tramore Races in mind. Racegoers used to treat themselves to First-class travel. You could at least go home in comfort on the return half even if you had 'lost your shirt'.** H C Casserley.

Above: **Bredin-designed gangwayed Composite No 2117, still looks well in the black-and-tan livery on 5th June 1964. Built in 1936 for suburban use, it had a three open Third class (now Second) sections and five First class compartments with a side corridor. The gangway was not original.** Derek Young

CORAS IOMPAIR EIREANN – THE GREAT AWAKENING

For the first few years, CIE was busy creating its new corporate image, most notably by the intensive use of paint. In the modern age of take-overs and mergers, fortunes are spent on engaging designers of what are now called logos. Interested parties like the writer could not condemn CIE for this practice, since engines, rolling stock and structures had been badly in need of paint for a long time. The 'flying snail' logo came straight from the other major constituent of the new organisation. The Dublin United Transport (nee Tramways) Company had been using this device since the early 1940s, but the green of their livery had been of a grassy hue. Now steam locomotives were given this colour too, something previously restricted to the three GSR giants of the 800 class. Since this was De Valera's Ireland the colour had to be green, but nobody objected, for green had been an engine colour since the dawn of steam. CIE's ivy-green with black and white lining was used also for coaching vehicles and the monotony of overall green when applied to carriages was pleasantly relieved by bands of paler green along top-quarters and waist panels.

Thus it was 1951 before the prototype CIE coaching stock emerged from Inchicore works, a series of side-corridor Composites and Seconds 60ft over body. This length was increased to 61ft 6in in the 1952 batch that included five vestibuled Seconds built for CIE by the still-independent GNR Board at Dundalk, on underframes sent from Inchicore. The Composites were to the same plan as the last GSR-built carriages of 1937, with end vestibules and three First class and four Second class compartments separated by two lavatories almost centrally situated. I am informed on good authority that the GNR drawing office had sketched out a similar arrangement many years before but the then manager, Bagwell, had rejected the plan that gave the lavatories 'the best seats in the train'. In the case of the new side-corridor Seconds the same plan was used, though the toilets were separated by a central vestibule and the 1952 composites sensibly repeated the latter feature. Publicity for the Irish tweed industry was assisted by the use of that fabric, under the brand name of 'Tintawn' (which means fireside), and the turf-coloured tweed looked pretty but it had not the hard-wearing quality needed for carriage upholstery and was soon replaced by conventional moquette.

A series of AEC railcar units almost identical with the GNR 600 class of 1950 began to come on stream in 1951. Numbered 2600 to 2659 they ran in pairs and were capable of hauling two intermediate carriages. Some interesting combinations of new railcars and elderly intermediates were to occur. From 2648 to 2657 a 'suburban' variation of the design was produced by omitting the lavatory accommodation. Later, capacity was increased by substituting bus-type seats, an unhappy downgrading of what had been a very popular design. Further alterations were made to the entire class as dieselisation of the Dublin commuter services proceeded, and before the 2600s (and the GNR 600s series railcars acquired during the 1958 share-out) had completely worn out, several had been de-motored and used as push-pull sets with a diesel locomotive. The last two, delivered in 1954, were one-class only for the Waterford & Tramore section. Conventional carriage construction continued in 1953, the Second-class open coach being introduced, sounding the death-knell of the archetypal side-corridor main line carriage. A batch of 14 Buffet cars was also produced at this period.

When O V S Bulleid commenced his 'retirement job' with CIE in 1954 there were inevitable changes including the use of that unpleasant Malachite green that had already overwhelmed both Southern Railway and Southern Region of British Railways. There were also were interesting developments in basic carriage construction. Several previously built coach bodies were mounted on the triangulated type of underframe used by British Railways under their Mark 1 coaches and 1955 saw the arrival of 50 sets of prefabricated parts from the Park Royal factory in London that were made up into lightweight coaches. These made full use of the Irish loading gauge by being a maximum 10ft 2in wide, this dimension being reduced to 9ft 6in at each end. The construction was, to say the least, unconventional, a blend of aluminium with steel and absence of a conventional underframe produced a tare weight of 26 tons. The thin outer skin of aluminium was spray-painted with an insulating compound on the inside. It is interesting to note that these coaches had inward-opening doors operated by motor-car type handles that confused the travelling public (the people who today rail about old-fashioned slam-lock carriage doors) to such an

extent that they were soon replaced by conventional doors. The Park Royals seated 82 Second-class passengers. A main line version with two lavatories seated 70, increasing tare weight by rather more than a ton.

The 10ft 2in coaches that followed in 1956 , Second class opens again, had more conventional underframes but the bodies were aluminium sheeted and timber-framed, the latter being laminated, glued and in one piece like a giant croquet-hoop, doing away with the long-established roofsticks. When seen stripped-down in the shops, they were 20 years old and looked flimsy indeed but appear to have given good service. There was 3-and-2 seating accommodating 70. The basic design was repeated in 1958 and 2-and-2 seating gave good room for trolley services, though it has been pointed out that tables were not added until later. A Composite version for suburban use retained the 2-and-2 seating for First class while Second class passengers were expected to sit three-and-three, which was asking a bit-much of the ten-foot width. The aluminium panelling of this era like the cladding of the new diesel locomotives, was the basic livery, on which was applied insignia and lettering in light green. But untreated aluminium can discolour alarmingly and locos and coaches alike received green paint once more (one of several shades used since 1945) after new stock came out painted green in 1958, the year in which Bulleid finally retired

In the early 1960s, CIE's railway system was going through its own version of the 'Beeching years' as the network contracted, the western and south-western counties suffering the worst depredations. Inchicore's ongoing programme of rolling stock renewal was the one bright spot in an otherwise barren landscape. The works were completing the long run of wide-bodied open Seconds for main line use. Production of these ceased in 1960, but revolutionary changes were in the pipeline, leading to the introduction in 1964 of the Craven coaches. In the intervening years building of more conventional coaching stock, when body widths reverted to 9ft 6in, kept Inchicore busy. Most notable were two catering vehicles the lavishly appointed Dining car No 2402 appeared in 1961. In 1964 came the first Kitchen car to be built as such, No 2403. A similar vehicle had been inherited in the GNR share-out in 1958. It proved very useful on special workings and was the probable reason for

Above: **In the early days of the new regime: a train from Amiens Street enters Bray on 10th April 1950. Engine No 672 is smart in its green livery and the old carriages also wear their new colours. But there will be sweeping changes before the end of the fifties.**

Below: **Perhaps CIE's 1950s main line stock might have been called, 'Mark 2 Bredins', as they had much in common with their GSR predecessors. They were warmly welcomed by travellers even though their new tweed upholstery was not a success. Here, the final touches are** being applied to new steel-panelled side-corridor Third No 1349 outside Inchicore carriage shops on 2nd June 1951.

building another. No 2403 went straight into the Radio Train rake enabling hungry excursionists to be fed without having to leave their seats. However, it should be noticed that an earlier conversion, No 29D, a former DSER bogie vehicle, was withdrawn from stock at the same time. Main line composites of the 1960s had side-corridor First class compartments and open Second class accommodation, an arrangement adopted by the GNR several years before. There was also a pair of First class saloons with 2 and 1 seating, air-conditioning, double glazing and fluorescent lighting. These coach bodies had traditional timber framing, flush panelled with sheet steel. Underframes were now made to the new 'triangulated' pattern, and the use of Commonwealth bogies must be mentioned. The latter were first seen on the Park Royals. They originated on the Pennsylvania Railroad and were manufactured under licence in the United Kingdom. Externally most noticeable were the equalising beams and coil springs; the former were finished in aluminium paint. Bogie frames were in cast steel, in one piece and roller-bearing axleboxes were used. CIE went in for the Commonwealth bogie in a big way, extra pairs being ordered for selected existing carriages. There was a significant livery change for coaching stock early in 1962. Green was out. In its place was an interesting combination of black, white and golden brown (in some circles called 'Black and Tan') that turned out well aesthetically. The writer recalls his horror at reading that County Donegal carriages were painted black when the Joint Committee was in dire financial straits, but black (for roofs and upper panels) worked in very well with brown and a white band where the old 'top quarters' would have been. This livery has survived for many years, only recently being overtaken by the arty-crafty colour schemes applied to cosmopolitan coach design at the turn of the twentieth century.

In the days of steam traction carriage heating was mostly taken for granted by the railway traveller. Come 1st October every year, our termini were wreathed in low-pressure steam escaping from the hose-connections between carriages. Each compartment had its simple on-off valve something like a small regulator handle, and a ribbed iron heater in the dusty recess under the bench seat on that side. No flow-and-return here; what steam reached the last carriage was dissipated into the atmosphere and the locomotive obligingly provided constant replenishment. When the diesels came, that was a different matter. Wealthier undertakings like British Railways equipped their new motive power with oil-fired boilers to do the same for thousands of carriages requiring steam heat. CIE, with delivery of their Metro-Vick A and C class diesel locomotives imminent, came to the conclusion that this would be unduly complicated. The heating van was the expensive answer. From 1955, Inchicore turned out an armada of 56 four-wheelers, 30ft long and built to the 10ft 2in car-

riage profile. The first 41 were sheeted in unpainted aluminium to match the finish of the diesel locos. They tared 21 tons and used the new design of triangulated underframe, under which were slung tanks for water and fuel oil, jostling for position with the accumulator box and dynamo. A Spanner boiler, first installed in the AEC railcars and capable of generating 1000lb of steam per hour, was situated in a small middle compartment with the Guard's van on one side and luggage space plus another water tank on the other. There were gangway connections. Four further heating vans of 1964 were 30ft six-wheelers (shades of past times) and weighed 30 tons. Two Spanner boilers gave double the output of the previous vans. Space was limited, with two fuel tanks underneath, accumulators were inside the van, along with two 500 gallon water tanks. Weighing as much as a bogie coach, the six-wheelers had roller bearing axle-boxes. The motley collection of pre-amalgamation luggage and parcels vans began to thin out in the 1950s, being superseded by a series of 66 luggage vans to the same dimensions and outwardly similar to the heating vans but with two sets of double doors. They had Guard's accommodation, corridor connections and their tare weight was a mere 10t 5cwt. More imposing were the ten vestibuled bogie vans of 1961, 61ft 3in long and 9ft wide, with the central Guard's compartment favoured by CIE. The venerable Post Office vans began to be honourably retired around this time. First replacements were ten 30ft four-wheel sorting vans, which one might not have regarded as a complete improvement on the old six-wheelers. They were externally similar to the previous aluminium vans but 9ft wide. A further seven TPOs were 60ft bogie vehicles fitted with lineside exchange apparatus. All these had toilets and tea-making facilities. With the exception of horse-boxes and carriage trucks whose use was declining in the second half of the last century, 'other coaching vehicles' had been brought up to date.

The next phase of carriage development on CIE began with the coming of the Cravens' coaches. Cravens Ltd, one of the foremost rolling-stock manufacturers in Britain (alas, where are they now?), contracted with CIE to supply 40 all-metal coaches, the first ten to be complete and the remainder as body-shells and bogies, fitting out to be done at Inchicore. These coaches were all open Seconds with extra-wide double-glazed windows. The bodies were aluminium alloy on corrugated steel floors, surfaced with plywood and compressed cork. Bodysides were insulated by glass-fibre packing between inner and outer panels. Much use was made of laminated plastics for internal finishes. The Dunlopillo seats were supported by tubular steel frames. Did not the GNR do this on its pioneer flush-panelled stock though without the foam-rubber? The two toilets were at one end of the coach and there was fluorescent lighting and a built-in loudspeaker system. Seating capacity was 64,

overall dimensions were 62ft 8in by 9ft 6in. Most interesting was the adoption of BR B4 type bogies, whose performance over lengthy trials in Britain was so striking that CIE accepted them without further trial in Ireland. They outmatched even the improved Commonwealth bogies.

The Cravens having proved themselves, a further 15 (in equal quantities Standard class, Composite and Brake-standard) were assembled at Inchicore and entered service in 1967/68 and a further 50 pairs of B4 bogies were obtained for use under earlier coaches, especially catering vehicles. The flow of new passenger stock then moderated due to implementation of a large programme of specialist wagon building to serve the new industries springing up in the Republic. The recently-built four-wheeled Post Office tenders had not been a success and were converted to luggage vans while three bogie TPOs were rebuilt from passenger stock. These TPOs were built without mail-exchange apparatus, signifying the end of the rather romantic 'pick-up and set-down at speed' practice that had lasted for more than a century. As the 1970s approached, further policy changes included a ban on using four-wheeled heating vans on fast trains. Ten double-boilered bogie heating vans were ordered from the Dundalk Engineering works that had taken over the old GNR shops. The Dundalk-built vans were Dutch-designed, built to metric dimensions that translated as 44ft 3in over headstocks and 9ft wide. The twin Spanner boilers were served by water and fuel tanks of 986 and 390 gallons capacity respectively. Opinions on train heating would soon be in a state of flux. The next move involved a substantial order to BREL (British Railways Engineering Ltd), who converted no less than 22 surplus BR Mark 1 coach bodies into steam-heating vans, these being equipped with the usual Spanner boilers along with diesel generating sets for electrical boiler heating, replacing the accumulators and axle-driven dynamos used previously. As there was room to spare in the bogie vans, space for the Guard and luggage was also provided. How simple the old use of steam from the locomotive now seems. BREL had by this time obtained a large contract for Mark 2D body-shells that would appear on CIE as the 'AC' (air-conditioned) stock. The first part of this order was a Dining car that arrived with the heating vans on board one of the North Sea train ferries. These vehicles made the sea journey to the North Wall on European standard-gauge bogies and were lifted on to the quayside by the Port of Dublin's 100-ton crane.

This new rolling stock began to come ashore early in 1972 and the first set-train of AC stock began its trials in October of that year. Irish rail travel had undergone a remarkable revolution. The one disappointment was the enforced adoption of the British loading gauge, the Mark 2Ds being only 9ft wide over body (the ex-Mk 1 vans were 9ft 3in wide). Another was the seating in the ACs, which turned out to be less comfortable than that in the Cravens stock or for that matter, the Mark 2s on BR. On the plus side there were Pullman gangways and centre couplers, double glazing and of course air conditioning. Electric heating hinted at another change. Fluorescent lighting, introduced with the Cravens, was used, and all coaches were wired for sound, a mixed blessing. The types supplied were; six Firsts (42 seats), nine Composites (24/24 seats) and 36 Standard class (64 seats). All had a small brake compartment and the practice of providing luggage shelves in one vestibule was initiated. A new classification Kitchen-standard covered 11 coaches with 30 standard-class seats and a kitchen and meant that meals might be ordered and eaten at any seat in the train. A surprise announcement was the abolition of First class from 4th December 1972, the deplorable title 'Super Standard' being adopted instead. The advantage was that this could be obtained for a supplementary payment of one Irish pound for each single journey. Who was to know that rampant inflation was just round the corner. The order was completed by a further 11 heating vans, also of Mark 2D profile, but now reclassified as Electric generator vans. Each contained two diesel generators providing power for lighting, heating, cooking and air-conditioning. Electric cooking was another radical change and saw out the propane gas that had superseded oil gas not all that long before.

If a picture of Inchicore works on a twenty-year marathon of mass production has been implied by this rather euphoric account, it is not wholly correct. Hard-line trade unionism on Irish railways has frequently been disruptive and destructive; much time was lost and many a programme slipped badly in those otherwise busy years. This has been partly responsible for the decline of Inchicore works, for many decades Dublin's largest industrial complex. A second factor was the radical change in coach-building practice and there was no chance of state assistance for the remodelling of carriage shops that would be required to facilitate this. In fact, a joint venture involving just that between CIE and a German rolling-stock manufacturer was given short shrift by the Republic's government, and this only a short time before Ireland joined the European Community. The buying in of components, a practice that began with the Park Royal stock, has reduced Inchicore to a place for assembling and fitting-out imported rolling stock.

Thus, with passenger traffic increasing and a shortage of stock becoming acute as the old wooden-bodied bogie coaches became life-expired, CIE once again turned to BREL for a further 100 main line coaches. Fifteen years after the Mark 2Ds had arrived, new Mark 3s came on stream from Derby. All 100 coaches had been delivered by the first weeks of 1988. Most were Standard class through there were also some Dining cars, Generator cars and First class coaches. The Super standards' had not been an unqualified success. Much custom had

been lost from businessmen who must have taken to private transport. First class accommodation had been retained on the joint cross-border services and was well-patronised. In the decade of make-do and mend there had been much regrading of coaches and the idea of 'Executive' class travel began to take root.

Bad luck and carelessness, to say nothing of malice, combined to write off new rolling stock in a series of accidents, the worst of which was the Buttevant derailment of 1980. There was fire-damage on occasion, including a malicious incident in September 1991 in an Inchicore carriage shop when a TPO was destroyed and Mark 2 stock damaged along with the refurbished veteran State Carriage 351. The Dublin suburban services were loaded to capacity. As a stop-gap when plans were being made for the Dart electrification, 'pushpull' working was introduced using former DMUs of 1950s vintage as driving trailers. The practice had been introduced for the Belfast-Dublin service by NIR in the 1970s. CIE would do the same in rather unusual circumstances. From a Northern perspective, lines in the Republic had been enjoying de-luxe treatment for years. Now CIE went cross-channel in the manner of the GNR in 1947, this time to a scrap merchant in Leicester whose yard contained a quantity of BR Mark 2 air-braked stock. Enough for a couple of push-pull sets arrived in Dublin by road-ferry on low-loaders and went to Inchicore still on their 4ft 8½in gauge bogies, which were converted to broad gauge. There must have been an element of barter in this transaction as the low-loaders returned to England laden with redundant CIE diesel locos. The requisite number of driving trailers were fitted out at Inchicore.

The last decade of the twentieth century witnessed a further re-arrangement of the Irish transport administration. A new body, Iarnrod Eireann (IE), was responsible for railway operation in the Republic. It was marketed as 'Irish Rail' at first. What was, in the author's opinion, their best badge so far began to appear on its trains, with the initials IR displayed in the form of converging railway tracks. This was short-lived, the Gaelic culture reasserting itself with a new totem, an IE monogram resembling a supersonic aircraft. The basic orange-brown, white and black livery has survived.

A return to the use of diesel multiple units was signalled in 1991, the order being placed in Japan. At this time surviving Park Royal coaches fell into disrepute and were banned from certain routes. All had been taken out of service by 1994, the year of the arrival of the Japanese DMUs. These were intended for outer-suburban and short-distance routes and further examples have since arrived from the Alsthom works in Spain. The push-pull mode was still in favour, more stock coming in 1995 from BREL in Derby before it was engulfed by Adtranz. Attention was at last turned to the Dublin-Belfast services, where EC money has helped to update the old GNR main line. This included the joint purchase of locomotives

and coaches, 28 of the latter providing two 'Enterprise' sets for each authority. These vehicles were built by de Dietrich of France to the current standards of main line travel, being delivered between May 1996 and March 1997. So far, everything in this book has been described in the Imperial notation used when the coaches were built. There is now no escape from metrication, and the quoted over-all length of each de Dietrich coach is 23 43 metres, or rather more than 76 feet. This is well beyond the record set by the GSWR's Rosslare Boat Train stock 90 years ago. The push-pull arrangement, inaugurated on the 'Enterprise' by NIR, with a diesel loco at one end and a driving trailer (DTV) at the other, has been perpetuated by the new trains. The consist is: DTV with First class seating for 30 and a luggage compartment, all-First with 47 seats, Catering car, four Standard class. One Standard in each rake has wheelchair accommodation, reducing seating from 71 to 68. The Catering car admits both classes but First class passengers may be served at their seats. The external livery is quite subdued, a sort of greyish mauve. In the years since its introduction the de Dietrich stock even though festooned with electronic gadgetry, has not won unlimited praise. At the time of writing IE is seeking tenders for 100mph passenger stock. This is 160 kilometres per hour and perhaps looks less alarming when quoted in mph. But passenger traffic on IE has a rosy future. Would that the same might be said of rail freight in Ireland.

Some of the BR designed CIE/IR coaches and the new stock for the Belfast to Dublin service are illustrated at the end of the last chapter in this book. They are Irish broad gauge carriages in the sense that they now run on the 5ft 3in gauge but their parentage lies elsewhere and they are not vehicles that were originally designed for use in Ireland. These carriages for example, do not make full use of the more generous Irish loading gauge. The last coaches to do so were the Craven built carriages of the of the 1960s (see page 44). Look at the profile of an ex-BR Mark 1 van at the end of a rake of Cravens to see what I mean (see page 95). These imports are included in this book the sake of completeness, but banished to its margins for this reason.

Opposite page, bottom:

The lightweight Park Royal coaches were revolutionary and though the design was not perpetuated the type had a long life, going through many internal changes in the process. This example is fresh out of shops on 12th April 1955, its number has still to be applied. A distinctive feature of these coaches is the way the bodywork narrowed from 10ft 2in to 9ft 6in at the end. The carriage is equipped with Commonwealth bogies which are finished in aluminium paint.

Top: **Another new CIE coach, Composite No 2124 of 1950, is seen in Boston sidings on 12th April 1952. These side-corridors had a central pair of lavatories dividing the three First class compartments from Third class. The latter are Seconds by now but the '2' has yet to be applied.**

Right: **The silver or aluminium decor of this 'hooded' four-wheel van, seen at Kingsbridge on 20th April 1957 was intended to match that of the new Metrovick diesel locomotives. After a few months in service, vehicles thus treated did not look so good, and another shade of green was adopted instead. Neither was the reversion to four-wheeled vans a great success; they were soon prohibited from running in fast trains.**

Top left: **One of Bulleid's four-wheel heating vans, No 3131, on a middle road in Sligo station, on 8th June 1957. By that time of the year, the carriage-heating season would be over. Note the Guard's compartment and the amount of equipment that was carried, both inside and underneath the van. The vehicle is in the aluminium livery which was also applied to CIE's new Metropolitan Vickers diesel locomotives when they first entered service. It would have been hard for CIE to find a less practical livery than this. The silver finish got filthy in a very short time, as No 3131 demonstrates so vividly**

Centre left: **The Craven built coaches were attractive looking from outside and comfortable to travel in, using the B4 bogies that had superseded the Commonwealth type. Here is Second No 1519 when new, seen at Cork Glanmire Road on 13th July 1964.** Derek Young

Bottom left: **The four-wheel Post Office vans of the 1960s were not a great improvement on the six-wheel veterans they replaced. One of the new vans, No 2963, is seen at Wexford North on 14th July 1964.** Derek Young

Bottom right: **Another example of the new types of stock which CIE was introducing was Heating van No 3153, one of a batch of six-wheelers, massive things that tared 30 tons and had roller-bearing axleboxes, which was recorded on 23rd July 1964.** Derek Young

THE GREAT NORTHERN RAILWAY

Many people regarded the Great Northern as a 'model' railway, in so far as it had achieved a creditable level of standardisation in the half-century between its formation in 1876 and 1925, which saw the amalgamation that gave birth of the GSR. In this respect it is worth quoting the doyen of railway writers, E L Ahrons who wrote, 'Of all the leading Irish railways, the Great Northern was probably the most interesting from the point of view of the varied designs of its locomotives and rolling stock, and the complete absence of the drab dullness engendered by modern standardisation'.

That was how the GNR looked to outside eyes in the latter part of the nineteenth century. We envy Ahrons for being able to see the variety of carriages the company had inherited from its constituents, but the outward uniformity of GNR rolling stock as it developed following Park's appointment as Chief Locomotive Superintendent in 1881 was nei-

The pride of the Great Northern just before the Great War, as new S class 4-4-0 No 172 *Slieve Donard*, built in 1913, poses with the Dublin-Belfast mail train. Prominent is low-elliptical Travelling Post Office No 9 (N1). The rest of the train is formed of clerestory stock, beginning with a W1 Guard's van, an F1 Composite, a Centre-kitchen Diner and another Composite followed by an M1 bogie van. Several Thirds, whose passengers were denied access to the diner, bring up the rear. The Green Studio.

ther dull nor boring and well deserves detailed scrutiny.

J C Park came to Dundalk from the other Great Northern at Doncaster, bringing with him some of the hallmarks of the English company's loco and carriage lineaments, including the round-roofed locomotive cabs of the Stirling family and the apple-green engine livery. For carriages, the 'house-style' my generation grew up with was initiated in 1882. New workshops for locomotives, carriages and wagons had been built at Dundalk in 1880, replacing the two establishments of the DBJR and INWR. From here emerged those mahogany liveried carriages that distinguished GNR trains up to 1958. Park's first productions were his standard six-wheelers built up to 1896. They had flat roofs and Doncaster practice was followed in the style of panelling; inset above the waist, while below, the surface was finished flush. On this were applied rounded mouldings of inch-and-a-quarter width, double at waist level to enclose the distinctive serif-lettering, blocked and shaded. This proclaimed company initials, coach number and class designation. On more modern coaches the bottom horizontal moulding was omitted, possibly to allow rainwater to be thrown off. All mouldings and window frames were square-cornered. Other companies rounded off corners in the hope that they would be less prone to take moisture. In early days it was common to apply elaborate monograms of company initials, though this was discontinued when costs escalated, but even in the final years of the Great Northern Railway Board the coat-of-arms was regularly applied,

the word 'Board' replacing 'Ireland' on the enclosing circlet.

One cannot be sure whether the varnished mahogany of that first period had the same hue as in later years. Mahogany may, like teak, vary from tree to tree. The former can be described as a rich reddish brown. Teak, as favoured by the English GNR, is the colour of golden syrup. Did Park use teak at Dundalk? Neither timber has ever been cheap, and economies had to be made. Whatever hardwood was used between the wars for new-build and repair work was obviously treated with mahogany stain, grained, scumbled and combed by the craftsmen at Dundalk. The writer recalls some older coaches being repainted at the Adelaide wagon shop during the Second World War and the result was like treacle.

In the six years from 1889 to Park's death in 1895, six flat-roofed bogie coaches were built. Five of them may be regarded as experimental (only the first two were identical) and no doubt went into main-line service as they came out of the shops. All were First-second composites with lavatories except the last, Trio No 404. It is doubtful whether they ran as a set train. The sixth vehicle was No 7 of 1892, a 45ft Royal Mail van. The passenger carriages all lasted until the 1950s, having been stripped of their lavatories after 1916. While the above vehicles were being built a very superior bogie Saloon, No 400, emerged in 1893. This was the first coach to have the 'low elliptical' profile that was another characteristic of the English GNR. It achieved Royal status at the time of the 1897 Irish tour of the Duke and Duchess of

Above: **With the purlieus of Dundalk works all around, VS class No 206 *Liffey* and the up 'Enterprise' negotiate the famous Square Crossing while the distinctive chattering of rail-joints passes down the train. Varnish on engine and coaches noticeably reflect the signal cabin.**

Below: **With the branch to Ardee trailing in on the left of the picture, GNR V class compound No 87 *Kestrel* sweeps through Dromin Junction south of Dundalk with an up express from Belfast to Dublin in the mid 1950s.**

York, and after static duty at Amiens Street terminus as accommodation for the Railway Transport Officer during World War 1, No 400 had a long career as a Brake-and-parcels van on the Belfast to Derry route. It became a signal fitters' van in the mid-fifties and continued on this duty when acquired by CIE in 1958. All the above stock were built to the 8ft 9in width like Park's six-wheelers and this was adopted for the remainder of the 'LE' designs, building of which continued until around 1901.

It is time to mention the system of carriage classification that has delighted GNR enthusiasts. Its mysteries were revealed in a card-backed booklet issued to staff. The earliest edition seen by the writer is dated 1916 but it may have originated before this. There was a cast plate affixed to each end of a coaching vehicle that gave class, length, width over body and tare weight. The class letter was followed by a number indicating the individual type.

As the number of six-wheelers dwindled rapidly between the wars, the letters O and P were later re-used for additional eight-wheel classes. Here is a list of the classes denoted in the 1916 book.

Bogie Vehicles:
A - Saloon
B - Dining car
C - First class
D - First-brake
E - Second class
F - First-Second Composite.
G - First-Second-Brake
H - Second-third composite
I - Tricomposite
J - Tricomposite & Brake
K - Third class
L - Third-brake
M - Guards'-brakes
N - Post Office sorting vans

Six-Wheel Vehicles:
O - Saloons
P - First Class
Q - Second Class
R - First & Second Composite
S - Second & Third Composite
T - Tri-Composite
U - Third Class
V - Third-brake
W - Guards'-brakes
X - Mail, Parcel & Vans

Four-Wheel Vehicles:
Y - Parcel Vans

The 1944 edition had O representing First/Third & Brake, actually slip coaches, and P for bogie parcel vans. S had become blank in the six-wheel list.

Charles Clifford, who succeeded Park as Locomotive Superintendent in 1895, developed the new carriage style and introduced the clerestory roof on a lavish scale. What may have been Park's last design - it was a low-elliptical 45ft breakfast car for the Kingstown Pier to Belfast service (it returned from the northern city as a tea car), was built in 1895. The car, No 338, was an unvestibuled side-corridor vehicle with a luggage boot at one end and a small kitchen at the other. Off the corridor were two each of conventional First and Second class compartments with external doors, where 'moveable tables' were installed when required, for patrons would occupy the same seats during the journey of approximately three hours. There were lavatories at either end of the side corridor. Clifford soon replaced 338 by a proper Dining car, No 401. This was a clerestory-roofed 50-footer accommodating 12 diners of each class on either side of the central kitchen. It was followed in 1896 by No 402, a 12-wheeler with 12ft wheel-base bogies and a body length of 55ft. In addition to dining accommodation for 12 of each class, a half-compartment at either end was labelled 'smoking' and provided the only means of access for intending diners. There were also lavatories for both classes. Neither car was vestibuled when built. Their successors, No 427 of 1900 and 457 of 1905 were marshalled between a centre-corridor First-second and a Second-third, the latter having an open Second class area and Third class compartments. As virtually all the GNR's bogie stock lasted to 1958 it is possible to make an educated guess as to which types were involved. Vestibuled clerestories of the classes F1, F2, F3 and F5 would qualify and the unusual design of Composites H1 (LE) and H2 (C), both with open Second and compartment Third classes, could have been used. Third class passengers were admitted to Second class dining areas on payment of a supplement, though until 1911, when corridor connections were first fitted to main line Third class stock, this had to be done by dismounting and re-boarding at stops. Official photographs of these first dining saloons show their beautiful finish to perfection. And Clifford did build his car bodies of Honduras mahogany. The last of the earlier saloons to be mentioned was No326 (A1) of 1900, with a 45ft by 9ft body which was selected to be the King's Saloon in Edward VII's Royal Train of 1903.

Construction of more prosaic stock to the low-elliptical profile continued to 1901 and included the K1 100-seater Thirds with 51ft 3in by 8ft 9in bodies, of which 18 were built. There were also sundry Composites and Trios that continued the tradition of through coaches from Dublin and Belfast to towns on the long secondary lines. From then on, clerestory stock of all kinds continued to be built until around 1910. The clerestory itself followed the English GNR's practice of being rounded off at the ends. In the period of post-war depression these glazed clerestories were all canvassed over to reduce maintenance and created a ceiling-scape of cavernous gloom.

The natural progression of design was towards the high-elliptical roof profile, but before this occurred a diversion from 1905 to 1907 produced a series of steam railcars and trailers with segmental roofs and 9ft 6in bodies with modified panelling. The steam cars were of the self-contained type and when the inevitable conversion to trailer cars took place the complete frame and body length was available for rebuilding. The North British Locomotive Company built three cars with bodies from R Y Pickering, Manning Wardle built a further four, with the Brush Electrical Co.supplying the bodywork. The nine matching trailers came from Pickerings. These trailers had a successful later career being used in the push-pull mode for many years, especially on the Belfast to Lisburn services. This operating practice came to an end after the collision involving a BCDR auto-train near Ballymacarrett Junction in January 1945, which rather put the Irish companies off push-pull working until well into the diesel era at least. Afterwards, these roomy cars were useful for excursion traffic but the scarcity of cross-partitioning in the bodies contributed to their comparatively early withdrawal.

A sad tale must be told concerning the side lookouts used on GNR Guards' brakes up to 9ft in width. These lookouts were handsomely designed, curving out in a graceful ogee to rise vertically meeting a capping piece sloping from the top window moulding. The Guard had a padded seat inside the lookout. In the late 1940s the load on an open wagon of a goods train shifted as it passed a passenger train on the opposite road. It struck the lookout and killed the Guard. This tragedy resulted in a decision to have these projections removed as vehicles came into shops. The programme was never finished and several Brake vans ended their days retaining one or both of their lookouts.

Close examination of the official booklet (it was entitled, Classification of Coaching Stock) reveals the progression from clerestory to high-elliptical stock as well as the ambiguities created when coach bodies were widened from 9ft to the final standard of 9ft 6in. Appropriately, we will use the GNR abbreviations to track this process. We start by adding an extra letter not mentioned before, 'V' which stood for vestibuled. On the GNR this referred to the corridor connections between vehicles, irrespective of an actual vestibule at the coach end. After a transition period when the 8ft 9in width of 'LE' stock was retained for some clerestory types, 9ft bodies became common in the first years of the twentieth century. The change to 'HE' roof contour came just as Dundalk was completing a batch of eight-compartment. K3 clerestories, the centre compartments of which had a curious 'dovetail' that made for two partially-concealed half-seat lengths, popular with generations of courting couples. The K3 bodies were 48ft by 9ft (25¼ tons tare), and 19 of these were built between 1904 and 1910. No 84 of that year came out as K4 and its 'HE' roof reduced tare weight to 22½ tons The same modification may be seen on other types. A solitary Third-brake L3 (C), No 350 of 1905 was repeated, apart from the roof, as L4 (HE), a class built from 1910 to 1912. As the 9ft 6in

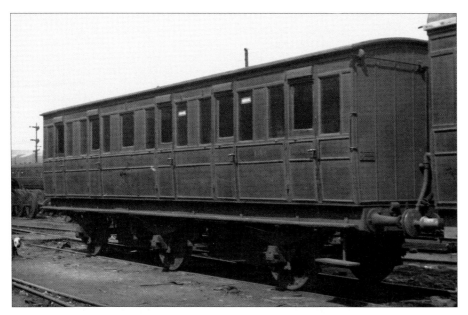

A Second class six-wheeler seen in branch line use at the end of its life. It was built in 1894 with a lavatory that served two of its five compartments. Removal of the facility increased seating from 48 to 52. The body dimensions were 33ft 6in by 8ft 9in. This vehicle was withdrawn in 1949.

stock was now coming on stream, there were further anomalies. Two of the last clerestories, Nos 15 and 38 of 1910 were 53ft by 9ft G1 Brake-firsts, semi-open with a centre gangway. They were followed by G2(HE) No 2 of 1911 having the same dimensions and plan, but vestibuled. That year HE(V) No 40, the singleton K5 introduced the open-plan Third class with a lavatory to GNR patrons. Strangely, this was still 9ft wide and its 52ft body accommodated only 64 Third class in eight sections of 2+2 seating. Another 'loner', K6 No 261, improved matters (as far as the company was concerned) in 1915 by being 56ft by 9ft 6in over body and held 90 passengers in 3+2 seating that became the norm for open ThirdS. One cannot find much affection for the K6 and its many successors; I was introduced to them on the 8.25am Derry train that always seemed the only one available if you had business 'out west'. It went from Platform 2 in the original Great Victoria Street station, which was against the south wall of the train shed. We sat in semi-darkness, the wooden floor still wet from its wash-down with a solution of Jeyes' Fluid, while outside the cleaners gave the train its final scrubbing.

It must have been good housekeeping by the building up of timber stocks that allowed Irish railways to continue carriage construction during World War One. The GNR, like the GSWR, was able to introduce new main line types. A Dining car (class B1) appeared in 1916, using the new length underframe. Its kitchen was at one end, adjacent to the 15-seat First class section. Second class seating for 19 was at the further end. Clearly, First class diners had a better chance of warmer food.

The GNR board of directors do not seem to have gone in for ostentation, perhaps they put the good of the company first. There had no doubt been a Directors' saloon in the six-wheel era, but it was not until 1911 that a bogie saloon for their sole use was built. It was relatively modest; while having a 9ft 6in wide body

this was still only 48ft long. There was armchair seating for 24 people in two saloons with a lavatory in between and a covered observation platform at either end. A removable ladder gave access to track level via end doors when required. The saloon A3 No 50, is one of the few GNR carriages to have been preserved. After refurbishment and repainting in GNR railcar blue and cream as part of the joint GNR/UTA Royal Train of 1953 it retained that livery until the end of its active life and now resides under cover at the Ulster Folk and Transport Museum. No 50 was joined in 1916 by an Officers' saloon (A5, No 144) on the new 58ft underframe. Photographs of this vehicle are rare, but it is reputed to have had open end platforms as one would expect. Perhaps it was deemed to be a luxury, for it was converted to a Dining car (B53) and went through a long history of change that was not uncommon for GNR catering vehicles.

The story of the GNR vestibuled open Thirds might well be called 'variations on a theme', construction lasting from 1911 to 1928 and involving classes K5 to K10. This also introduces us to the Tea cars that represent another milestone in GNR catering. The service they provided began in September 1914, the three K7 class of that year being built with a kitchen at one end of the coach. In the case of No 28 this was 10ft 6in long and there was a side corridor. Nos 34 and 41 had a kitchen so small that perhaps galley would be a better name for a space that was 4ft 1½in long and tapered in width, as the passage from the centre gangway to the vestibule connection had to be slanted. What space remaining on the other side was made into a pantry. Cooking of what have been called light meals was done on an oil stove. The Tea cars were first used on trains between Dublin and Belfast running outside the hours of regular meal times but did offer food to Third class passengers, served to their seats on trays. But there were no tables. Tea cars appeared on the Derry Road and the Irish

North during the 1920s. The last of the Tea car came in 1932. They were evolving into the Buffet cars, developed enthusiastically by the GNR and CIE after the Second World War. They were all listed in the 1944 edition of the Carriage Book but ended their GNR careers with pantries and kitchens replaced by 3+2 seating of the modern tubular kind. The writer never had the opportunity of sampling one, but wonders what those light meals were. Sandwiches bread and butter, scones, barm brack, soda bread, none of these need the services of an oil stove save to brew the tea or coffee. Could you get a boiled egg, or tinned soup? Whatever one's opinion of an Ulsterman (remember the GNR mostly served the Nine Counties) he will not take offence at being told that he is fond of his grub. One's memory of GNR catering is High Tea, the Ulster Fry of course, plus the trimmings, or that chicken dinner in the immediate post war years when chicken was still a luxury to most of us.

One of the last of the wood-panelled classes was the K13 of 1932, a marked improvement on previous Thirds with open 3+2 seating. Nine K13s were built, and had side corridor and eight and a half compartments to seat 68. They had a lavatory at one end and a curious cubbyhole at the other. They were to be looked for on the Derry Road for they gave smoother travel over the bouncing boglands of Tyrone. The K14 Tea cars laid down at the same time also had the side corridor. Flush-panelled stock had already appeared when the very last coach with wood panelling and raised mouldings was built in 1936, the open Third No (K19), with 60 seats in a body 43ft 6in long, special for the Banbridge to Scarva line. Like some other 'Ks' No 3 had a small brake compartment that should have qualified it to be an 'L', as well as a luggage compartment at the other end that had been a feature of the very first bogies of 1889.

Production of the flush-panelled (sheet steel) main line stock began in 1935 with F1 side corridor Composites for the upper classes (seats 24/24) and K15 open Thirds sensibly made to have 2+2 tubular framed seating for 70 passengers but with the usual one lavatory. The K15s, centre-gangwayed of course, were in nine divisions, four of which had doors on each side with the usual quarterlights and the remainder with the large windows. This remained the standard arrangement for main line Thirds until the end. The alternative modern version of the side-corridor Third, still popular with rail travellers the length and breadth of these islands, was tentatively intro

Above: This was one of a handful of flat-roofed bogies built by J C Park. No 404 was the only Tricomposite and seated 16 First, 20 Second and 40 Third class passengers. Classed I10, its dimensions were 46ft by 8ft 9in. Latterly it was stationed at Clones, where it is seen on 15th July 1957.

Below: No 392 (F10) was a Luggage-first-second also built to the old profile in 1892, which had lavatories for both classes. These were long gone when the carriage was seen on a returning excursion at Bangor on 3rd June 1950. The Health & Safety people would have hysterics at the porter nonchalantly waiting to couple-up the engine and stock.

Above: **No 398 (F11) was another variation, though the size of the luggage compartment suggests that it had also carried a Guard when new. Built 1892, the 45ft by 8ft 9in body seated 16 First and 28 Second class passengers, No 398 was photographed on 26th September 1952 in Great Victoria Street carriage sidings in Belfast.**

Centre left: **An early picture of flat roofed TPO 7 (N2) of 1892, whose body was 50ft by 8ft 9in. Renumbered 487 in 1916 and 789 in 1924, it was kept as a reserve vehicle and eventually scrapped in 1950, having lingered round the works yard for many years.**

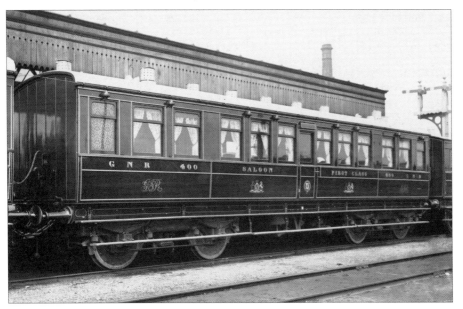

Bottom left: **First class saloon No 400 is superbly finished for the Royal Train of 1897. Note that it has oil lighting and that safety chains were still de rigeur. The use of Laycock's ventilators along the top panelling is uncommon.**
Charles Friel collection.

duced in 1936 when two 64-seaters (K17) were built. A further two were added in 1945. There was still only one lavatory per coach. Classes L12 and 13 built at the outbreak of the Second World War seated 39 and had a van section 22ft long. Main line coaches with Guards' accommodation in the HE(V) era were notable for their generous van space that had wide sliding doors and inward-opening Guard's doors.

Fifteen K15s and five F16s would be built up to 1943, along with three Buffet cars and a Diner, all in the new mode, making for trains of uniform appearance. Hauled by the sky-blue Compound locomotives, the new trains caused a great stir on the east coast, as well they might. Three new Brake-composites (J11) for the through workings from Derry brought some modernity to the north west. The J11s had an open Third section for 30 plus a lavatory while First and Second class each had one compartment off a side corridor with one lavatory, and were were accessible from vestibule. Beyond this, the van was 10ft 2in long.

The Second World War, coyly referred to in the Free State as, 'the Emergency' found Dundalk works with sufficient material for several 58ft underframes and bogies. On these were built fifteen 'Workmens' coaches' (K23), which were sent north where they proved very useful in a period of heavy traffic. Despite their 'austerity' construction (and their slatted wood seats weren't all that bad either) the external finish of narrow hardwood strips, tongued, grooved and v-jointed, suited the GNR livery. As soon as conditions improved the K23s were put through the shops and emerged as K15 and L14. Two were made Buffet cars, reusing the K23 mark that was also given to two conversions from K15s. The finest years of the GNR, only a decade from the end of its existence, were about to begin.

Cross-border services were still thriving as the wartime traffic in the north fell away. The idea of non-stop running between Dublin and Belfast, with Customs examinations taking place at either end, arose. By mid 1947 a seven-coach rake of new and refurbished stock had been assembled. It catered for First and Third class only. The new service called the 'Enterprise Express' was inaugurated on 11th August 1947, leaving Belfast at 10.30am and returning from Dublin at 5.30pm, with a journey time of two and a quarter hours. It was warmly welcomed by the travelling public who for years had endured the lengthy, double Customs examinations at Dundalk and Goraghwood. A second set was available in the following year allowing two expresses each way on weekdays. Train formation (from the Dublin end) was: D5 brake-first, C2 First, K24 Buffet, three K15s and an L14. The C2 was particularly attractive and built to the postwar standard length of 60ft ¾in (60ft underframe). The arrangement was: end-door, gents lavatory, three compartments, centre vestibule, three compartments, ladies lavatory and end door. It seated a total of 36. The success of these trains put CIE on their mettle and in 1950 the 'Enterprise' was extended to Cork, there being a stop-over for Customs examination before the train was shunted from the GNR terminus to the adjacent Amiens Street Junction station, and vice versa. The GNR had to suffer the overnight loss of its best rolling stock until CIE was able to assemble a scratch combination of Bredins and vintage GSR coaches and work turn-about with the GNR. The through running of the 'Enterprise' to Cork lasted to mid-1953. By that time CIE was in a position to display its own 'modern image'.

In 1948, the Dundalk coachbuilders were putting the finishing touches to the last two C2s when the writer was given a conducted tour of the works. The astonishing sight of crimson-liveried LMS bogie coaches occupying a large part of the carriage shop was enough to divert ones attention from those exquisite C2s. Short of carriages, the GNR had purchased a bargain lot of former LNWR corridor stock, 20 in all. Life expired they may have been by the more exacting standards of BR, but they were to prove to be very useful on GNR secondary services. The Wolverton-built stock encompassed the LNWR profiles of flat, cove-roof (equivalent to low-elliptical) and high-elliptical, occupying GNR classes G7, K25 to K28, L15 and O2. The LNWR had for years built coaches miserably narrow even by standard-gauge parameters and some of these imports were only 8ft 6in wide. Most were 9ft, but the two flat-roofers had underframes so narrow as to foul 5ft 3in bogies on sharp curves. Cutting pieces out of the bulb-section LNWR solebars was considered but found to impair their structural integrity. They ended up as lineside huts. Existing bogies on the remainder were adapted to Irish gauge. On the general subject of coach bogies, it should be mentioned that Fox's pressed steel type were used at first, in common with other Irish lines. Wheelbase was 8ft until the advent of 9ft 6in wide HE stock, which had 10ft wheelbase bogies. The latter will be recalled as having 'fish-belly' side frames. When the GNR flush-panelled coaches were introduced, the first few K15s came out on old standard underframes with tensioned truss-rods. The new design had angle-iron trusses and bogies of the built-up type, rivetted or welded, using LMS drawings courtesy of the NCC drawing office but with the lengthened wheelbase.

There was a further chapter to the second-hand saga in 1951. The DNGR had closed and its nine remaining Wolverton built six-wheelers came into the GNR list. The old livery was retained. They turned up on excursion trains but after a couple of summers most were relegated to Departmental stock.

Mail Vans and Slip Coaches

Travelling Post Office vans were well established between Dublin, Belfast and Londonderry before 1876. What must have been an interesting group of six-wheel TPOs (some with gangways), built between 1877 and 1887 was joined in 1892 by Park's flat-roofed bogie van No 7 with 45ft by 9ft body. The six-wheelers, later classed in the X series, had mostly gone by the 1920s. No 7 became class N2. N1 was represented by a second sorting van, No 9, with a LE roof contour and 50ft by 9ft body, built in 1901. It was burned at Castlebellingham in 1922. By this time sorting vans had been renumbered in the 700 series, the N1 becoming 788 and the older van No 789. A third TPO, No 790, had been built in the same year. It was a magnificent beast, 58ft by 9ft 6in with a HE roof, quietly slipped across the border when completed as there were now two separate postal authorities in Ireland, albeit sharing the same framework of activity. No 790 worked a Portadown-Derry mail service with mail pick-up apparatus en route (though not presumably in that portion of the Derry Road between Strabane and Derry which passed through the Free State?) until July 1927. At this time No 789 must have been a spare vehicle. On cessation of this service both vans were retired to Dundalk works. No 789 was officially withdrawn in 1950. No 790 lay alongside the carriage shop for several years and even had a protective coat of grey paint before she was scrapped in 1954. There was talk of making her a luggage van, but when our guide on a works visit was asked about it the quick reply was, 'Oh no, that belongs to the British government.' It was there in case the GPO, as it then was, ever decided to reinstate the Derry TPO.

This is as good a place as any to make brief mention of another GNR amenity; the provision of sleeping accommodation on the night mails that lasted from a round 1908 to 1918. It involved little more than conversion of lateral seating in First class compartments into bunks. Three clerestory coaches were used, two of them I2 Tricomposites, the third an F13 First-second. The down night mail left Dublin at 8.20pm with 'sleepers' for Derry and Belfast. In the up direction accommodation was on the 9.30pm ex-Derry which Belfast to Dublin passengers joined at Portadown. The down Belfast coach returned to Dublin the following day, though what happened to the bedding is unclear. The charge was 5 shillings (25p) per berth on top of the First class fare.

Most of the major Irish companies toyed with slipping carriages from express trains to make connections with intermediate towns or branches. The GNR was the last and possibly the most extensive user, having 14 of its Brake-ended bogie coaches adapted for this practice. The Appendix to the Working Timetable details fitting of a special slip coupling to be made at the last stop before the point of slipping. The slip Guard had to bring the coaches (the maximum was four) to a stand using his handbrake only. The drawback of slipping was that the process could not be carried out in reverse and made for a rather unbalanced timetable. Examples were slipping at Drogheda for the Oldcastle line and at Lisburn for Portrush. That was a summer working, an enterprising piece of co-operation with the LMS(NCC). The last pair of slip coaches to be

Top left: **The experimental breakfast car No 338 (shown here at Adelaide on 7th June 1960 as N301 of the UTA), retained a semblance of its appearance though altered internally to a one-off Composite class F6. These alterations produced the notorious smugglers' compartment, boxed-in empty space at one end.**

Below left: **Unvestibuled 52ft Brake-tricomposite No 57 (J10) had lavatories for superior classes only and a 7ft 6in brake compartment. Some of these early low-ellipticals had elaborately paneled ends, although spoiled by steps, handrail and alarm signal in this case. These were given the mahogany treatment at first, but all coach ends made do with black paint in later days. This view was taken on 17th May 1952 at Sutton, the Hill of Howth tram depot sidings are in the foreground.**

built were classed 01, being (unusually) Brake-first-third. By an odd coincidence, class 02 appeared in 1948, an ex-LMS(LNW) LE double-ended Brake-composite of 1907, itself a former slip coach. Its new number was 470. The two Guard's compartments were very small and the GNR made one of them a luggage bay. Other, indigenous, slip coaches were of classes G1 (2), G2, J1, J2 (3), J4 (6). The practice was discontinued on the outbreak of the Second World War and was never restored.

When work on this review began, a conscious decision was made to exclude diesel railcar development and concentrate on loco-motive-hauled stock. But as the idea of multiple-unit working took shape these two disciplines became harder to separate and we must refer to the GNR's contribution in this field. Its system became a proving-ground for evaluation (without expense) by the newly formed British Transport Commission, of operation by multiple-unit railcars. By the out-break of the war, the GNR had successfully introduced a range of single-unit and articulated railcars for branch line and suburban use. The only other company in these islands to

take this matter seriously seems to have been the Great Western Railway, working in conjunction with the Associated Equipment Co. Ltd. of Southall, Middlesex and the body-builders Park Royal Vehicles Ltd. The GWR had a fleet of 34 single-unit cars when in 1941 it took delivery of two 2-car sets capable of hauling an intermediate coach when required, and at express speeds. Nationalisation in 1948 interrupted further progress, but almost coincidentally the GNR, whose officers had been following events in Britain, placed an order for 20 such units with AEC. The 20 AEC/Park Royal cars were delivered in 1950. Numbered 600-619 in the coaching stock list, they operated in pairs and had the capacity of taking an intermediate coach. The front of each car was occupied by the Driver's compartment, a glazed screen separating it from the First class section to create what was almost an observation car with 2+1 seating for 12 passengers. Beyond was lavatory accommodation and a 32-seat open section for Third class, with space for the Guard and luggage at the rear. Body length was 62ft 6in. The Guard's compartment of each even-numbered car contained a Vapor-Clark-

son oil-fired heating boiler. For main line service the intermediate car was a K23 Buffet, otherwise K15 open Thirds were adapted for use with the railcars. The distinctive 'Oxford blue and cream railcar livery was applied. An ordinary carriage was occasionally added as a trailer, highlighting the capacity shortcoming of such units that are noticeable to the present day, when spare coaches seem to be non-existent. But the 600s were immediately popular. Traffic patterns also demanded a two-car set formed by a motor car and a trailer. This need was met by construction of the last two Dundalk-built coaches, classed K31, in 1954. They were basically K15 vestibuled open Second with driving compartment and were numbered 8 and 9.

What the GNR now needed was 'more of the same'. Instead, faced with a financial crisis on 1st September 1953 both governments found themselves unwilling joint owners of an undertaking now styled the Great Northern Railway Board.

The new body had to plead its cause for new rolling stock. It took literally years to obtain further 24 railcars, the 701 and 901 classes. The last vehicles were not delivered until the GNRB was on the point of being divided, in the manner of King Solomon's judgement, between the two nationalised transport undertakings. Cars Nos 701-716 were Second class units and Nos 901-908 were Composites something similar to the 600s but without luggage accommodation and having a wide vestibule at the inner end. The 12 First class seats were tiered to give an unrestricted view ahead. There were separate lavatories for First and Second class, the latter section seating 40. The 701s could be driven from either end. Gone was the panoramic view. Each end had vestibule connections of the German tubular rubber type; on either side of these was a lav-tory and a Driver's cab. Passengers were contained in one long section with vestibules and doors at either end seating 56. Both types might be 'mixed and matched' so that up to four power cars could take a further four ordinary coaches. The first three 701s were used to make a substitute rake for the original steam-hauled 'Enterprise', only with six coaches instead of eight. They were arranged thus(note the arrival here of the unsatisfactory phrase power car'): Power Car (56 Second class), C2 (36 First class), B9 Buffet (24 Second class), D5 (16 First class), Power Car (56 Second class) and finally another Power Car seating 56 Second class passengers. The guard was now almost in the centre of the set in the enlarged brake end of the D5 and with a Spanner boiler for company. Hence the loss of one First class compartment in the D5. Total seating was 52 First class and 192 Second class. Lay persons might have wondered at the necessity of carrying five unused and presumably expensive sets of control equipment in that ensemble.

These last GNR diesel sets had been manufactured by British United Traction Ltd, successor to AEC, whose engines had been increased in capacity and horsepower. Bodies of all-metal construction by Park Royal Vehicles, came as kits of parts to Dundalk Works, where the last vehicles of the protracted order were completed by the Dundalk Engineering Co., state-sponsored to take over railway work and other commercial ventures that included the short-lived construction of a type of Bubble Car, of the road rather than rail variety! I have been fortunate in finding in the issue of *Modern Transport* for 15th June 1957 a full technical description of these cars. I have never really thought this august weekly to have been pro-railway, but here it paid a well-deserved tribute to the GNRB: '*Although the Great Northern Railway Board cannot be said at the moment to have an assured future before it, that situation cannot be laid at the door of the undertaking but must rather be attributed to the indecision of the governments of Northern Ireland and the Republic of Ireland with the scarcely hidden indifference of the former as the strongest influence. Had the necessary authority been forthcoming when it was first needed, last week would not have seen demonstration runs... but, instead, completion of at least a year's running by the last cars built under the programme. It verges on the tragic that the railway which in the British Isles pioneered the use on a substantial scale of multiple-unit diesel trains should have been prevented from benefiting from an extension of their operation.*'

Six-wheelers and Four-wheelers

Between the two editions (1916 and 1944) of the Coaching Stock Classification book, inroads had been made into the stock of six wheel passenger vehicles. Only three Seconds were left and the nine Tricomposites were divided between five sub-classes, two of which had luggage compartments. There was only

one Brake-trio. Six Brake-thirds and 30 Thirds could be seen on sidings between Belfast and Portadown, kept for workmens' trains which served the Lockheed aircraft factory at Gortnagallon. This was reached by a short branch off the Knockmore Junction to Antrim line. The stock used on these trains was notorious for the punishment it received from its clients, who were being paid more than they had ever before received in their lives. Some of the standard six-wheel Guard's vans were useful survivors. Of 27 built between 1889 and 1896, six were given new bodies around 1944 with vertical sheeting in the style of the K23 'workmens' coaches. The three clerestory vans (W1) built to match the Mail Train in 1904/5 had gravitated to branch line service but were well-kept. Concerning the 'X' classification for parcel vans, the motley collection of 1916 that included a foxhound van, one which housed a vacuum cleaning equipment and various stores vans, had dwindled to one example, X5 No 782, a parcels van that survived on the Bundoran branch in a woebegone condition up to its closure in 1957. Others had been taken out of the carriage stock but were still around in odd corners to surprise us. One pair of six-wheelers must be mentioned even though they were scrapped in 1925. The GNR acquired them on taking over the Belfast Central Railway in 1885. They appear in a well-known view behind a BCR tank engine somewhere on that wayward little line, and were built in the style of the Railway Carriage Company of Oldbury. Given the GNR Nos 373 and 374, they were 45ft long over body and ran on Cleminson's radial gear, which allowed the centre wheels some movement on curves thus explaining their great length for six-wheelers. As they differed in the number of Second and Third class compartments they had, the punctilious GNR gave them separate class numbers, T2 and T3.

The four-wheel parcel vans, classes Y2 to Y9, were always in great demand, even by the UTA, who rebuilt some rather brutally with horizontal sheeting. They came with flat, low- and high-elliptical roofs and plenty of louvered ventilation. The 10 parcel vans of class Y5 were built by the Société Franco-Belge in 1912. Class Y10 of 1920 covered three motor car vans which had HE roofs and double end doors, naturally enough. In side elevation they were very similar to the Y6 vans of 1915. The GNR horsebox was the one type of coaching vehicle not to have a class letter, yet their associated carriage trucks took classes Y11 and Y12. The horseboxes were allocated the numbers 601 to 700 in the coaching list and all these were occupied at one time or another, some more than once. A large scrapping programme depleted their ranks in the years around 1940, when redundant bodies (still bearing numbers) were distributed around the system for static use. Last to be built were a batch of eight in 1939/40, more utilitarian than the old ones. Of this earlier design (the diagram is dated 1885) three remained in 1958 of which CIE got two. The newer horseboxes were divided

equally between CIE and UTA. There were 20 out of 39 carriage trucks left in the 1950s, all being rebuilt as Y13s for Guinness traffic. Four tranship trucks that exchanged containers with the Donegal system by means of the mixed gauge turntable at Strabane were included as coaching stock though all had gone by 1938.

The vans of classes Y7-Y9 had a confused history, all being numbered in the goods wagon list to begin with. Classes Y7 (1901) and Y8 (1895) covered ten refrigerator vans, later brought into the 800 series as coaching vehicles. They are noted as having treble-sheeted floor, sides, ends, and roof. They were 18ft by 8ft over body, rather low-built, with partitions making an 18in space at either end, presumably for ice. Remembered as being an unusual 'desert sand' colour, they were to be seen on a siding at the outer end of Grosvenor yard in Belfast. Some were drastically rebuilt to produce the peaked-roof luggage trailers towed by the early diesel railcars. The rest were converted to fish vans (of class Y9) around 1952. These totalled 51 in 1958. They were 15ft 2½in by 8ft on a 9ft wheelbase, with high-level ventilators each side of a double door.

At the end of the GNR alphabet, class Z1 appeared in the 1930s under the title 'Refreshment Vans', copying an idea of the GSR. Indeed, it is said that Dundalk sent someone to take notes of what seemed to be a successful ploy. So the GNR gutted three old 'W' vans, fitted them with vestibule connections, shelves down each side and a portable bar at one end. They were said to be seatless but one wonders how many customers of the 'advertised excursion' were horizontal by the end of their trip!

One four-wheeler remains to be mentioned, a Tricomposite with two decks and numbered 381, the celebrated Fintona Horse Tram. It is fortunately still to be seen at Cultra. The tram (Fintona folk called it 'the van') was built by the Metropolitan Railway Carriage and Wagon Company in 1883. As everyone knows, Third class passengers were supposed to use the open top deck. The saloon was divided in two for First and Second class, but was used by all in wet weather. The able-bodied preferred the upper deck, no matter what ticket they held.

When the GNR was formed in 1876, it inherited a total of 379 coaching vehicles from its constituents. These were as follows; First class, 31, Second, 25, Third 101, First-second composites 73, luggage, brake and mail vans 68, horseboxes 40, carriage trucks 37, Post Office sorting vans 4. The UR contributed the greatest number of coaching vehicles, a total of 123. Eighty-two years later, passenger-carrying stock (including Guards' brakes) were numbered between 1 and 500. Withdrawal of older bogies coaches and the last six-wheelers left about 340 passenger carriages in that series, including the M vans. Other coaching vehicles occupied numbers 601 to 790, with gaps. The GNR could be proud of those years of orderly development.

Above: **The 10-compartment K1 bogie Thirds seated 100 passengers in a 51ft 3in body. Most of them employed on the Belfast to Portadown services were badly treated by their users. Some of the compartments were covered with unrepeatable graffiti when I travelled in these coaches back in the 1940s. No 429 is at Antrim on 6th April 1957.**

Below: **This is the short-lived TPO No 9 renumbered 488 in 1916 and burnt in a 'Wild West' style ambush at Castlebellingham in December 1922. A particularly pleasant design, and well lighted, its classification was N1, the body was 50ft by 8ft 9in.** Charles Friel collection.

Bottom: **Mounted on six-wheel bogies, No 427 (B3) came out in 1900, intended for the morning up and evening down expresses. Again with a centre kitchen, the 56ft body had 15 seats in each class. Despite having a refit in 1946 it was scrapped in 1950.** Courtesy, The Green Studio

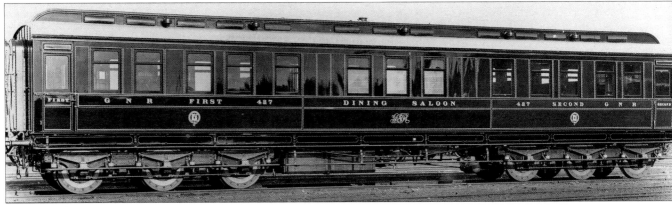

Top: **No 401 was the first conventional dining saloon built by the GNR in 1895. Gangways were added later. It was replaced in 1916 by a Second class dining saloon with a high elliptical roof and bearing the same number and classification.** Charles Friel collection.

Centre: **Classed as B1, 401 became 407 in 1916. In 1921 it was remodelled as an A2 class saloon and later still was converted to an E5 type Open Second. It became a dining car trailer during World War 2 and is seen here on 26th September 1952 as a First class saloon (complete with antimacassars) although bearing its E5 plates. It was scrapped soon afterwards.**

Above: **In 1905 a further 12-wheeler No 457 (B2) went into service, the last of the centre-kitchen type built for the GNR. This had 18 First class and 24 Second class seats of the tip-up sort. The body was 56ft long. Note that the primary purpose of the clerestories was ventilation; there are no glazed panels.**
Charles Friel collection.

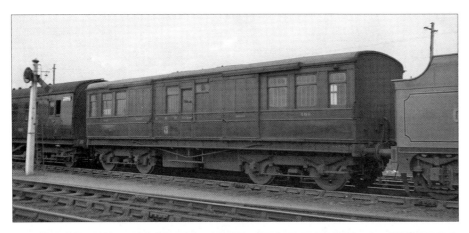

Left: **Still carrying the number 400, the former saloon is now an M4 passenger van, a regular performer between Belfast and Derry. Here on 9th July 1952 at Portadown the second vehicle of this down express is a J11 Tricomposite, built for use on the Derry Road.**

Below: **Seen in sylvan surroundings at Drogheda on 15th May 1954, G4 composite No 148 built in 1901 with a 45ft by 9ft body, was intended for through working between main line stations and long country branches but has first class accommodation reduced and lavatories removed.**

Below: **L1 Brake-third No 246 dated from 1904. Seen at Warrenpoint on 30th August 1958, it was one of only three vehicles in** its class which were notable because of the generous size of the brake van, which occupied 27ft of the vehicle's 50ft length.

Right: I12 Tricomposite No 356 built in 1904, was a curious conversion from a K3. The compartments were arranged 3.3.3.1.2.3.3.3, the middle half-compartment being divided between First and Second to give sub-standard comfort for both classes. The coach is seen here in the Cookstown branch set on 17th June 1950.

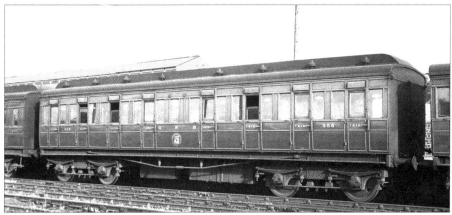

Centre: A familiar visitor to Strabane, M1 clerestory van No 456 is being shunted into the bay platform on 16th May 1959 where it will exchange parcels with County Donegal vehicles.

Below: The first three GNR steam railcars had 58ft by 9ft 6in bodies. They were later converted to J3 Tricomposites. In this broadside view the former rear driving position (now a Guard's compartment) is on the right. Inward-opening doors replaced lattice gates and additional surgery took place. Second class is at the left hand end. Remaining unvestibuled, they were useful as slip coaches with the Guard having a panoramic view. No 203 is seen at Newry on 20th July 1933. Charles Friel collection.

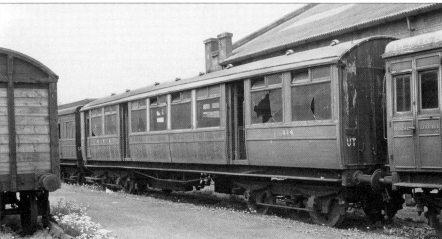

Above: **Push-pull trains replaced steam railcars, using matching open stock of segmental roof profile built by R Y Pickering & Co. F12 No 215, originally a Composite, now reduced to Third class only, was 53ft by 9ft 6in and is seen here in an excursion rake at Bangor on 6th June 1953.**

Left: **The Third class version of the above was the K9 class of 1906, with a 51ft long body. Seen awaiting disposal at Queen's Quay on 23rd July 1959 is No 214. This type had a shorter life than most GNR bogies, we are told that a lack of lateral bracing weakened the bodies.**

Above: **In 1904/5 Dundalk turned out three pretty six-wheel clerestory vans (class W1) to match the new sets of main line stock which was illustrated on page** 45. **They were 30ft long and electrically lit. Eventually, they gravitated to branch line work. Here is No 247, out to grass at Adelaide on 13th October 1959. The look** out **on the other side had been removed by this time. Another one of the class became a breakdown van at Portadown shed.**

Above: **The Directors' Saloon (A3) has been described in the text. For its role in the 1953 Royal Train which was a scratch assemblage of UTA and GNR stock, it was painted in the blue and cream railcar livery and retained these colours for the rest of its active life. The Saloon is seen at Great Victoria Street against the backdrop of Murray's Tobacco Factory on 16th June 1958.**

Right: **F2 class Composite 313 was a modern suburban coach dating from 1921 made all-First on abolition of Second class in 1951. Here it is on part of an Irish Railway Record Society special at Ardee in County Louth on 15th May 1954.**

Above: **The high-elliptical vestibuled Brake-trios of class J4 were useful through coaches that turned up at places like Newry and Warrenpoint. Seen in** Bundoran goods yard is No 64, awaiting its return trip on 29th June 1957. The J4s had a 13ft 10in Guard's van, two semi-open Firsts seating 12 and two 12-seater Second class compartments. The Third class section seated 21. They had a centre corridor and lavatories for all classes

Left: **Setting a trap for the unwary modeller, L114, a vestibuled Brake-open Third, was one of a handful of high-elliptical stock built around 1913 with a slight variation in the vertical panelling above the waist. The scene is again Ardee on that pleasant outing on 15th May 1954.**

Below: **The very last GNR wooden-bodied coach with traditional panelling was built at Dundalk in 1936. This was K19 No 3, an Open Brake-third for the Scarva and Banbridge line. This went to CIE in 1958. Repainted in green and renumbered C3N, it is in repose at Drogheda on the site of the original Dublin & Drogheda terminus on 18th May 1963.**

Left: **We have now reached the flush-panelled era. Here is open Third (now Second) No 81, a class K15 steel-panelled coach built in 1937, photographed at Amiens Street on 9th May 1959.**

Right: **The last of a long line of dining cars was B4 class No 403 of 1950, now cabled for intermediate use with AEC railcars and painted accordingly. Seen as UTA property at Amiens Street on 9th May 1959, it was later renumbered N554.**

Below: **K23 buffet No 188 was the intermediate car in the pioneer AEC railcar set 600-601. It is seen here as part of the formation of a special excursion from Dublin to Bangor on 2nd July 1950.**

Right: **No 470 was a 'cove roof' LNWR First-Third slip coach (note the Guard's compartment each end) acquired from the LMS and put into service in 1948 as Class 02. The Clones roundhouse is in the background in this 15th September 1957 view.**

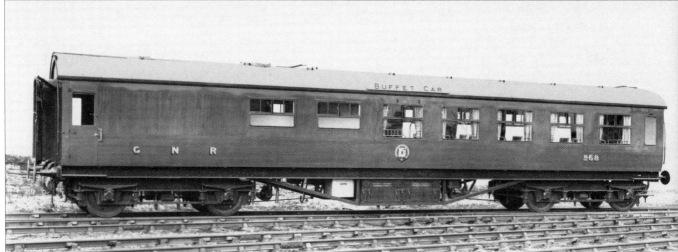

Top: **Migrant K27 vestibuled side corridor, a LNWR high-elliptical design. It had a lavatory at either end, unlike GNR carriages. It is awaiting attention at Dundalk works on 2nd May 1953.**

Centre: A B10 buffet car of 1950 in ex-**works condition. From 1944 all catering vehicles were designated buffet or refreshment.** Charles Friel collection.

Above: **Nos 272 and 399 were M2 bogie vans dating from 1901/2 selected for conversion to B7 class kitchen cars at the beginning of the Second World War. Their conventional panelling was modified as required. High elliptical roofs were also fitted.** Charles Friel collection.

Right: **The class K23 was the wartime series of so-called 'workmens' coach, built on standard underframes. The vertical hardwood sheeting can be seen on this official view of No 153. Used on services radiating from Belfast, 'utility' would have been a better title, though their wooden seats were superior to those on the contemporary motor-buses. After the war they were quickly converted to K15 and K23 buffet cars.** Charles Friel collection.

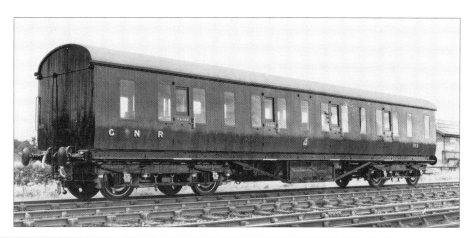

above: **Class M5 high-elliptical vestibuled bogie van is in CIE colours when on a special working at Antrim on 12th June 1964.**

Right: **Parcels van No 752 built in 1902, was the only member of the class Y2 and had been renumbered N641 by the UTA before the photographer tracked it down at Dungannon on 24th April 1961. It has suffered the loss of some basic mouldings that lessen the GNR style. Its basic dimensions were 24ft long, 8ft 9in wide and it weighed 8½ tons.**

Above: **The ventilated four-wheelers were more in demand. Here is No 764, of class Y5 of 1912 which was fitted with sliding doors, seen at Dundalk works on 2nd May 1953.**

Centre left: **The flagship of the Departmental fleet was No 8453 which toured the system demonstrating its contents to enginemen. These included models of valve gears and a portion of model railway with signalling. Converted from a standard six-compartment Third of 1882, it had a 30ft by 8ft 9in body and was painted in full passenger livery complete with a coat-of-arms. No 8453 is seen here at Dundalk Junction on 2nd May 1953.**

Bottom left: **The fully panelled W vans disappeared rapidly after 1945 but several could still be found in Departmental use up to the 1950s. Seven W2 six-wheel passenger brakes were rebodied between 1944 and 1946 with vertical sheeting, an inward-opening Guard 's door and a sliding door for merchandise. This example was re-sheeted by the UTA in its preferred form with horizontal planks. N604 was in Omagh goods yard on 29th April 1961.**

Right: **The last of its class, X5 six-wheel parcels van No 782 spent its declining years on the Bundoran branch, where it was recorded on 29th June 1957. The X series contained a host of six-wheeled oddities though all had gone by the time I began photographing GNR stock, except for No 782.**

Below: **Three PI class bogie parcels vans, of which No 780, seen at Bundoran Junction on 29th June 1957, was one, emerged in 1930. Another ten, similar but with steel-framed bodies appeared in 1944. The 'goods' construction may explain why the bogie wheels were only 3ft 1½ in diameter.**

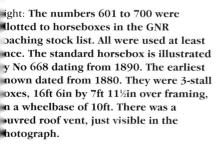

Right: **The numbers 601 to 700 were allotted to horseboxes in the GNR coaching stock list. All were used at least once. The standard horsebox is illustrated by No 668 dating from 1890. The earliest known dated from 1880. They were 3-stall boxes, 16ft 6in by 7ft 11½in over framing, on a wheelbase of 10ft. There was a louvred roof vent, just visible in the photograph.**

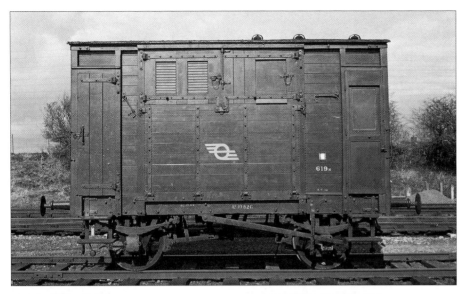

Top left: **A further eight horseboxes to a new design were built in 1939/40. The 10ft wheelbase was retained, body dimensions were 16ft 10in by 8ft 0½in. External appearance was much plainer; torpedo vents replaced the louvres and the doors to the harness compartment were without droplights. No 619N was in CIE green when photographed at Mullingar on 18th March 1963.**

Centre left: **Carriage Truck No 712 dated from 1883 and was listed as rebuilt in 1910. It was classed Y11 but there does not seem to be room for a plate. These trucks and boxes were painted what has been described unofficially as 'orange-brown'. This colour was also used for prize cattle wagons and Departmental stock. This being coaching stock, company initials and numbers are applied with transfers**

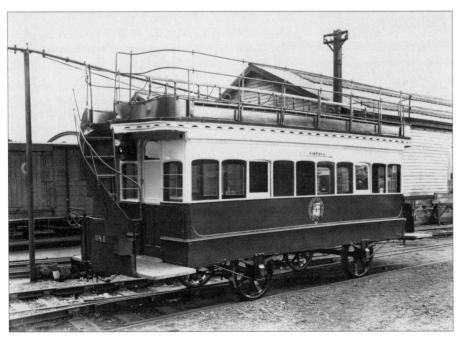

Bottom left: **This section would not be complete without a picture of No 381, the Fintona Horse Tram. We are not sure what the original Fintona 'van' looked like. The 1883 replacement, an enlarged version of a contemporary street tram car, was built by the Metropolitan Carriage & Wagon Company and was originally numbered, 74. It received the blue and cream livery in 1946. This official view was taken to record the damage incurred when poor old Dick, the horse which pulled the tram, bolted in 1953. Fortunately, this was far less serious than the press made out at the time.** Charles Friel collection.

FROM THE BNCR TO THE LMS

William Dargan was a busy man in 1847. He had secured the contracts to build both the Belfast & Ballymena and the Belfast & County Down lines, the former opening on 11th April 1848. The B&B was transformed into the Belfast & Northern Counties Railway in 1860 and by amalgamation and expansion became the foremost railway on the northern seaboard. Information on early B&B/BNCR carriages is scarce though some are said to have been built by Thomas Firth, a Yorkshireman who established a wagon-building works on the Falls Road in Belfast, an area of the city far from a railhead. Firth also acted as the Locomotive Superintendent of the BCDR from 1854 to 1861 and he was still wagon building in the 1860s.

More than 30 years of BNCR history are virtually blank as far as coaching stock details are concerned. Occasional gems surface, including the following account of a saloon carriage of 1862 discovered by the late George Mahon and published in *IRRS Journal No 35*. The saloon was built at York Road Works in Belfast, under the auspices of Alexander Yorston, the BNCR Locomotive Engineer at that time. There were two compartments; one held 22 persons on cushioned seating round the sides. The smaller of the two was a smoking compartment. It had taken a long time for railways to accept such a practice and what the BNCR produced would have done much to make an addict break the habit. We are told that there was a large mirror at one end and adequate ventilation to disperse the 'heated air'. There was cast iron open-work under the roof, where the top quarterlights would have been. This for a start would have produced a howling gale, but one end of the compartment was open. If this is taken literally, such a vehicle would need turning at the end of each journey and even then upholstered seats would have little protection from the rain. Perhaps the open end was a sort of observation platform.

The distinctive style of BNCR coaching stock that survived into the twentieth century was introduced in the time of Bowman Malcolm, that self made locomotive man whose reign lasted almost to the end of the Midland era. He may be called the Irish Daniel Gooch, for having entered the BNCR loco department at 16 he became its Superintendent in 1876 at the age of 22 and did not retire until August 1922. He lived on into LMS days, his death occurring on 3rd January 1933. Seen in elevation, the style of panelling used by Malcolm was pure London & North Western except that BNCR coach sides were vertical, without any waisting. This would have made them easier to fabricate. The well-proportioned panelling and crimson lake livery embellished with gold-leaf lettering and the borrowed arms of Belfast made for a handsome and recognisable series of vehicles. Not until old age, when mouldings were stripped off and sheet steel replaced wood panels, did the design look really woebegone. A total of 165 rigid-wheelbase passenger coaches are known to have been built in Malcolm's style between 1876 and 1892. Fourteen of these were four-wheeled Brake vans 21ft 11in by 8ft 6in over body, of which two survived until the 1940s. Of the 151 six-wheelers, four were First class saloons in two sections. One of these also had two lavatories. There were two four-compartment Firsts with 29ft 6in bodies, but the standard length adopted for six-wheelers was either 30ft 6in or 31ft 6in. Six Second-class carriages were altered to Third from 1905, but both classes had compartments the same length of 5ft 11in which was generous compared to those on other lines. Seventy Thirds and Brake-thirds were almost identical. Close observation revealed that one end compartment of five of the latter had double doors and one quarterlight. However, a dozen six-wheel full Brakes were available to make up any deficiency and 19 out of 51 Composites had centre luggage space, while there were five Brake-tricomposites for slip working. A Post Office van of 1883 was joined by another, converted from an 1877 Third, in 1901.

The prototype bogie coach was built at York Road Works in 1893. No 7 was a six-compartment First, 43ft 10in long and 8ft 6in wide to the same 'flat' roof contour as Malcolm's six-wheelers. (This was known as 'low roof' on the NCC). On its heels came Composite No 71 of similar dimensions with three First and three Second class compartments; one of each class had access to a lavatory. The underframe of No 7 was used for a new Post Office sorting van in 1934 while the composite was sold to the BCDR in 1943. Construction of two First class saloons for the tourist traffic in 1894 established the new standard length of 48ft 2½in and ushered in an era of excellent craftsmanship. Body width was to remain at 8ft 6in for a while. Fox's pressed steel bogies with an 8ft wheelbase were used under the new coaches.

The Saloon carriages Nos 8 and 9 had observation ends enclosed by ornamental ironwork. Internally, the bodies were in two unequal sections; one with two bays had a long settee on one side, curved round one end partition, and three revolving armchairs on the other. Two of these remained in situ when the body of No 9 was examined in 1964. The longer section of three bays had a dining area on one side with fixed seating and tables for 12. Another settee occupied the opposite side. A thoughtful touch, for summers on the north coast can be unpredictable, was a built-in umbrella stand in each saloon. The internal panelling was decorated with pokerwork in the fashion of the time. This had been executed skillfully by Bowman Malcolm's daughter. Beyond the dining area was a small kitchen. There was a lavatory at the opposite end of the coach. The open platforms were later vestibuled and gangwayed. This handsome pair were used on the Larne boat trains and on the 9.15am Portrush express in summer. Each seated 34 passengers but a percentage would have their backs to the window (an irritating feature of many Irish saloon carriages), the passing scenery being admired at the risk of stiff necks. No 8 was rebuilt in 1924 by being widened to 9ft 6in and given a high-elliptical roof; it became a Royal saloon on occasion and from 1941 to 1953 had one open platform restored, carefully covered in green canvas when out of use. It was enclosed again for the last time and refurbished as part of the Royal Train of 1953. It ended its long career in GNR blue and cream and with the UTA number 152. It was scrapped in 1964. No 9 was completely rebodied as a saloon in 1927 and the old body, became a summer bungalow at the Juniper Hill caravan park in Portrush. Until the site was cleared in 1964, Juniper Hill was a huge carriage and tramcar museum!

In 1895 York Road turned out a Tricomposite on the standard underframe having two each of First and Second and three Third class compartments, plus two lavatories. The design was repeated in 1899. The first of the type joined No 71 on the BCDR in 1943. In the meantime, a substantial order had been placed with the Ashbury Railway Carriage and Iron Company who delivered 20 coaches in 1896 consisting of 13 eight-compartment Thirds, four seven--compartment Thirds with lavatories and 3 Brake-thirds of the 'centre-van' type with two compartments at one end and three

Above: **No 471 was an early Bowman Malcolm 4-wheeled passenger Brake dating from 1878. On 18th April 1947 it was marshalled among wagons in Antrim goods yard. The housing on the end protected the bevel-gearing of the Guard's vertical brake wheel. Other appendages of the past are the pressure gauge for gas lighting, a couple of skylights on the roof and the door of the dog-box.**

Centre: **Malcolm's standard six-wheel Brake-third No 207 of 1884 was still gas-lit in the 1930s and has the Guard's double doors as described in the text.**
Derek Young collection.

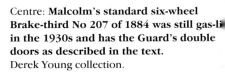

Left: **First class Saloon No 3 of 1886 seated 30 in two sections, disposed around the sides. A similar saloon used by football teams, had a toilet between the two saloons.**

at the other. York Road added a further three of the latter in 1899. Malcolm's last design of the nineteenth century was a Brake-tricomposite with lavatories. Eleven of these were built between 1897 and 1898. It was a long-lived design, much altered with brake ends enlarged, lavatories removed and the classes changed around.

The one BNCR carriage recorded as built in 1899 was a tour-de-force for the carriage department, Dining saloon No 10. While overall dimensions remained the same, there was a novelty in the clerestory roof as well as electric lighting. Being First class only (seating 32) the kitchen was at one end. The external finish was splendid. There were two external doors each side bearing a BNCR monogram below the word 'First' and centred between the doors was the company's borrowed arms and supporters with 'Dining' and 'Saloon' on either side in gold leaf, blocked and shaded. Harold Houston, in his comprehensive paper on NCC coaches (*IRRS Journal 35*) describes No 10 as having a vestibule connection at one end only. It is unclear whether this was to admit other first class passengers or to permitting dining car staff and stores access from a similarly-equipped Guard's van. At any rate, through gangways were added on rebuilding in 1926 to an 9ft 6in width and a high elliptical roof. Lining-out on everyday BNCR coaches was described as a ⅜in gold leaf stripe and a ⅛in vermilion line on all panels. Ends, buffers and headstocks were also lined. The saloon served lunch on the 12 noon Portrush express for two shillings (10 pence) and dinner on the return trip for three shillings (15 pence).

The clerestory era brought forth a four-coach Boat Train set in 1902; bodies were widened to 9ft and there was a centre-corridor lavatory First, a similar Second class coach and two eight-compartment Thirds. In LMS days the clerestories were replaced by HE roofs. In 1903 the BNCR was swallowed up by the mighty Midland Railway (England), yet things went on very much as before. Apart from the use of the (old) Midland coat-of-arms and 'NCC' in monogram or initial form, liveries remained unchanged. Local officers had great autonomy and there was no attempt to abolish second class! In the same year a new four-coach tourist train was inaugurated, a joint venture with Mr Holden of the Laharna Hotel in Larne. Four First class saloons were built for the exclusive use by Holden's tours, an itinerary that included 400 miles of rail travel, 40 of charabanc excursions and six days hotel accommodation, all for £2-7s-6d (£2.37½p). Layout was somewhat similar to the 1902 set, three cars being centre-corridor and the fourth a Dining car with end kitchen. Body size was now 52ft by 9ft 6in but the roof contour was again 'low'. There was a six-wheel Guard's van at each end of the set, fitted with one gangway. The Great War put an end to the tours and the coaches went into ordinary service, getting HE roofs in LMS days. An external feature that should be mentioned was the use of match-boarding for lower panelling, also found on other saloons like old No 9, of the Malcolm era. Miss Malcolm also was busy in the carriage shop, for her pokerwork decorated internal door panels of the 'Holdens.' One thinks this work was done in a seemly fashion, before the doors were hung.

Two steam railcars arrived from the MR's Derby Works in 1905. They were of the articulated type and, unusually, Tricomposites. In appearance, the coachwork was nothing like anything produced by Derby or York Road. Mouldings were round-cornered but there was no 'LNWR' resemblance. When the engine units wore out in 1915 the bodies, with some modifications, were made into Tricomposite-brakes. The small rear driving compartment now housed the Guard; the First class section remained unaltered, entered by a vestibule that also gave access to a Second class section seating 16. Beyond this, 49 Third class seats were distributed in two unequal sections on either side of another vestibule. It involved lengthening the car underframe and abolishing a luggage compartment immediately behind the power unit. These Tricomposites were now 55ft 22in long and 9ft wide, retaining their 'low' roofs. Numbered 79 and 80, they gave useful service into UTA days. This work concluded the NCC carriage programme for several years.

Bowman Malcolm had retired before Derby supplied 30 modern coaches of LMS design in 1924, though these had some interesting variations to cater for local requirements. These included six Tricomposite-brakes, five Tea cars having two First class compartments, two half-Firsts, three Seconds and one with a pantry, three Composites with two First class compartments like the Tea cars, and four Seconds. There were also 14 eight-compartment side-corridor Thirds with lavatories. A First class diner with kitchen, No 88, and Third class trailer diner, No 9, were distinguished by the new LMS coat of arms.

Body dimensions were now 57ft 1in by 9ft 6in, with HE roofs, This programme enabled withdrawal of six-wheeled stock to commence. York Road built its first coach to the new pattern at the same time, the prototype being a vestibuled open Third in two sections, seating 80. A total of 16 to this general design were built. New stock for the Larne boat train and general use were built at York Road up to 1935 using LMS components though not slavishly following either Derby or Wolverton in general arrangement. The latter workshops embarked on production of the famous 'Larne Steelers' in 1933, the NCC's first use of flush steel sides and steel roofs. There were Tricomposites, ten-compartment Thirds seating 120 (the latter were 60 footers) and eight-compartment Brake-thirds.

York Road's glory years were approaching their zenith. Contemplation of a fast commuter service between Portrush and Belfast crystallised into the famous 'North Atlantic Express' now that the Greenisland Loop had been completed. Five coaches were built for this service, including Buffet car No 90 seating 26, with a cocktail bar and kitchen; thus, one did not need to reside in Brighton to breakfast on the way to the office. The remaining four were side corridors with 5ft windows on both sides. These were a Tricomposite, a Brake-third and two seven-compartment Thirds. The Third class compartments had flush armrests, the kind that could be pushed back to allow four seats a side - remember the nasty people who refused to do that? The North Atlantic coaches were 60ft 1in x 9ft 6in. Internal finishes all along the train were of a high standard, with much polished mahogany. By 1937 the Railway Magazine could say, 'the speed of 58.1 mph (for 67½ miles with one stop) gives the NCC the blue riband for railway speed in Ireland.'

The North Atlantic rake is understood to have worked a turn to Larne Harbour and back during what would have been a long lieover in Belfast. In this context it is interesting to note that a replacement Brake-first for the Boat Train was built in 1937 to similar standards of comfort. This coach, No 7, was on the new 60ft underframe and was the first NCC vehicle to have Stanier's 4ft 6in wide windows with sliding ventilators. Work was now commencing on a new range of vestibuled stock, of which 30 were intended to be completed by 1940. Nine Brake-tricomposites were on the rails by 938 and a new class of open Thirds, with 80 seats in two sections, were under way when retrenchment took place. The economic horizon was uncertain but as Harold Houston noted, worse was in store for the NCC Operating Department who entered the Second World War with 12 new coaches less than expected. Before the nine open Thirds had been finished a managerial instruction saw these fine coaches made into 90-seaters using bus type seats. The folly of this decision was rectified in the middle of the war when in Houston's words, 'they became comfortable 80-seat coaches.'

By then disaster had struck yet had been surmounted. The NCC works and terminus were in a most vulnerable part of Belfast, separated from the strategically important shipyard area by only the width of the Lagan. Luftwaffe attacks in the Spring of 1941 saw 20 coaches destroyed in one night as well as much goods stock and severe damage to plant and buildings. The parent company reacted with commendable promptitude, by producing 20 57ft 1in x 9ft LMS ten-compartment Third class coaches which were shipped to Belfast. A further 24 coaches were dispatched in 1942, a fascinating variety of corridor and non-corridor types, all post-grouping stock, with both steel and wooden bodies. In this time of trouble the Irish railways closed ranks. The GNR was repairing NCC stock at Dundalk and the GSR's Inchicore works built wagons for the NCC. In passing, one also recalls a great number of ex-Midland wagons being re-gauged and sent over to the NCC at this time.

The NCC's last new carriage was something of a luxury. What later became known as the 'Chairman's saloon' (No 3) was a purpose-built 60-footer, reputedly one of a series built for LMS management, perhaps remembering the fate of Lord Stamp the LMS President, who with his family had been killed in the London blitz. The Saloon was described as having a lounge, three single-berth bedrooms, lavatory, an office with dining table seating six, a galley and attendant's lavatory. It was a mobile home and workplace for the manager but its arrival in the year of the invasion of Europe came rather late as Northern Ireland was by then relatively safe from attack from the continent. No 3 formed part of the 1953 Royal Train, but by 1959 had been gutted and converted to railcar No 56.

On 1st January 1948, the NCC found itself part of the vast national transport system that was British Railways, initially controlled by the Railway Executive. Happy to hang on to the railway steamship services, the British Transport Commission was aware of gathering trouble in Northern Ireland as the pre-war friction between road and rail re-asserted itself, with the defenceless BCDR bearing the first brunt of the attack. By 1st October the same year, the BCDR had become part of the Ulster Transport Authority, and with Major Frank Pope, former manager of the NCC, the UTA Chairman. The chief officers of the NCC locomotive and operating departments found themselves in charge of the railway side of things before the NCC officially merged with the UTA on 1st April 1949.

Loose Ends and Brown Vans

Taking notice of the GNR system of carriage classification, the NCC had introduced a modified version of this in 1933. The class plates were of enamelled sheet metal with numbers, sizes and tare weights handpainted. The plates appeared on each coach-end but were easily obscured by dirt, unlike their precursors whose characters were cast in relief. The identifying letters were; A Saloon first, B Dining car, C First, D Brake-first, E Brake-first-second, F First-second or First-third composite, G Tea car, H Tricomposite, I Brake-tricomposite, J Third, K Brake-third, V Passenger brake, luggage and other vans, bogie six-wheel and four-wheel and finally Z for all other six-wheel passenger vehicles.

In that same year, the NCC had another influx of rolling stock. That other LMS enclave, the DNGR, was embarking on a serious cull of surplus stock, both goods and passenger. The Greenore folk off-loaded three Third class six-wheelers and three bogie Brake-tricomposites that were found useful enough at York Road. All solidly-built Wolverton products dating from the turn of the century, the bogies immediately became Brake vans and while one would be lost in the 1941 blitz, the others saw service into the UTA era, readily distinguishable by their waisted sides. The six-wheelers had a good innings as service stock. There was also a typical LNWR horsebox and, most modern of all, a motor car van, with a high-roof, dating from 1906. The NCC's own horseboxes had dwindled since Malcolm's time. There had been 16 single (3-stall) boxes and 6 double (6-stall) horseboxes, built to designs introduced 1876 and 1885, all four-wheeled with falling sides counterbalanced by top-hung upper sections. Five carriage trucks were extant in 1940. Open wagons for pork traffic built in 1909 had the curious NCC arrangement of combined passenger and goods springing also used on cattle wagons. Some became container flats.

Seventy four-wheel fish vans were built between 1883 and 1896 but few, if any, survived the Second World War. These, and the later 'brown vans', were numbered in a 18XX series. There was always a need for parcel vans on NCC passenger trains that never seemed complete without a string of four-wheelers bringing up the rear. These long-wheelbase vans, 24ft over body, were introduced in 1928. Plain, practical and Presbyterian, they suited their Northern Counties surroundings very well. Their colour was LMS bauxite brown which soon changed to UTA passenger green at take-over but they retained their old title even in official circulars. A handful of six-wheel bread vans of 1915 went into general use along with the four-wheelers, whose total number reached 39. Many of their fleet numbers replaced those of the old fish vans.

Mention should also be made of the two ambulance trains formed during the war for use in Northern Ireland. Strategically placed at Whitehead on the Larne line and Broomhedge on the GNR main line, they each consisted of seven coaches three of which had been supplied for administrative use by the LMS and regauged. The NCC and the GNR each provided four coaches fitted out as a theatre car, pharmacy car, staff quarters, Dining car (one of these was NCC B1 class No 10), stretcher car and stores van. The ambulance trains were decommissioned in 1944, having fortunately seen little employment. Photographs of one of these trains appear in a companion volume in this series, *The LMS In Ireland*.

Below: **This 4-compartment First had been converted into weighbridge fitters' van No 3108 when photographed at York Road on 21st February 1951. The low winter sunshine shows Malcolm's panelling to good advantage.**

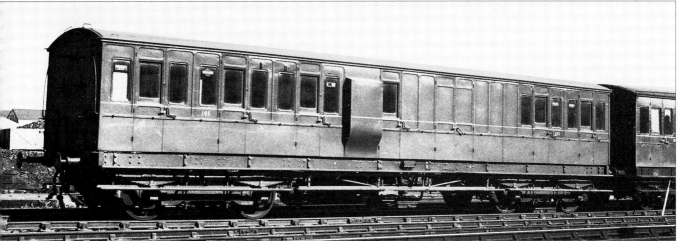

Top: **Lavatory-composite No 71 was the second bogie carriage built by the BNCR. Still gas-lit when photographed in 1936, electric lighting was fitted when No71, along with three other BNCR bogies, was sold to the BCDR in 1943. At the same time, the lavatories were removed. They were 43ft 10in long.** Derek Young collection.

Above: **One of six centre-van bogie Thirds, No 105, built in 1896, has been painted in UTA green, but still retains its original mouldings. Body length was 48ft 2½in, which had become standard. No 105 is seen at York Road on 13th May 1950.**

Right: **Tricomposite-brake No 1036, at Bangor on 22nd August 1952, was one of several older coaches that had 1000 added to their numbers to make room for new stock in the 1930s. Externally it is almost in 'as built' condition, the Third class has become part of the van and the lavatories**

Above: **Here is First class saloon No 14, built for Holden's train in 1903. It has a 52ft by 9ft 6in body. The verandah ends were later enclosed and a high roof was fitted in 1927.**

Centre left: **The dining car from Holden's train, No 13, was also modernised for general use in 1932, the end kitchen being made into a parlour (on the right of the picture). Note that these cars have had their under-frames re-trussed with fixed angle-iron members. Malcolm's use of vertical matchboarding on the lower panels of saloons can also be seen. The vehicle was photographed at Greenisland on 4th July 1951.**

Bottom left: **Unvestibuled bogie Thirds used on long distance services had lavatories. This is the former No 142, renumbered 327 by the UTA. This carriage was given its high roof by the LMS. Its lavatories had been removed in 1945 increasing its seating capacity to 78. The vehicle is seen on the scrap line at Queen's Quay on 26th March 1960.**

Above: **Four bogie Brakes of 1904 were rebuilt with 48ft 2½in by 9ft 6in bodies and high elliptical roofs by the LMS. Renumbered 407-410 in the 1930s, here is one of these, No 407, at York Road on 2nd May 1957.**

Top right: **A curious hybrid, bogie Brake No 402 was one of three rebuilt from DNGR Tricomposite-brakes in 1933. The LNWR low flat roof has been retained and the underframe and bogies are also pure Wolverton. Photographed at Larne Harbour on 29th June 1953, with mixed-gauge track in the foreground.**

Centre right: **The locomotive portions of the two Derby-built steam railmotors were worn out by 1914 but the bodies were useful and became Tricomposite brakes. Renumbered 79 and 80, and known as 'halt coaches', they lasted into UTA days. No 80 is seen at York Road in 1936.**

Bottom right: **Dining car No 88 was one of the first coaches built at Derby for the NCC in 1924. It looked rather shabby, seen here stored at Greenisland, between a BCDR six-wheeler and a bogie Brake. It was given the UTA number 160 and was withdrawn in 1972.** R S Carpenter Photos.

Top left: **A Restaurant car in less than pristine condition, this former Derby-built Tea car of 1924 was in the former GNR Adelaide locomotive yard in Belfast on 8th June 1963, carrying its UTA number 170. It had been officially reclassified as a Dining car by this time but it seems to have reached the end of the road. The presence of an elderly carriage here was a bad sign, few emerged from here for further service.**

Centre left: **A handsome vestibuled side-corridor Tricomposite-brake, No 33 was built at York Road in 1936 to the new 60ft length.**

Below: **A view of the compartment side of No 34 of the same class, carrying the UTA number 246. One of the last LMS coaches to be turned out with external wood panelling, it is seen at York Road terminus on 9th September 1964, by which time it was a Brake-first-second. D F Tee.**

Top and centre right: **Illustrated here are two of the three surviving North Atlantic coaches, acquired for preservation by the Railway Preservation Society of Ireland in 1975. They are seen here in service on a special working to Portrush on 11th September 1965. The coach in the top picture is side corridor Brake third No 91, renumbered 472 by the UTA. The other carriage shown here is Tricomposite No 92 (UTA No 240). The other preserved North Atlantic is Third No 94.**

Bottom right: **A sad view of No 430, the LMS TPO built in 1934 on the underframe of No 7, the first BNCR bogie carriage. Withdrawn on the outbreak of the Second World War, its whereabouts remained a mystery to this photographer until it appeared in an auctioneer's list in 1954. It was photographed in the former Dunadry goods yard on 14th August 1954.**

Above: The well-known 'brown vans', four-wheeled and with high roofs, were built at intervals from 1924 onwards and were numbered in the 1800 series. This example bears the UTA number 690 and has been tinkered with, using louvres and gauze for ventilation. Note also the steel underframe and modern axleguards. **Their bodies were 24ft long. Photographed on 21st May 1962 at Maysfields, the former-GNR goods yard beside the River Lagan, where Belfast Central Station was later built.**

Top left: A series of six-wheel bread vans built around 1915 were used latterly for general parcels work. This is No 1860, 30ft 6in long and painted bauxite brown originally but now green. Seen among the square-setts of Duncrue Street goods yard in the 1950s, the outside axleguards used on nearly all BNCR/NCC rigid axle vehicles are prominent. The same custom prevailed on the BCDR, as will be seen elsewhere.

Top right: Standard NCC horsebox No 469 awaits its fate at Dunadry on 14th August 1954. The design was unorthodox in several ways. Were these boxes built on second-hand underframes? We will never know, but the ends would withstand strain better with pillars bolted to the headstocks, like the double horsebox in the illustration below. The type was first built in 1876.

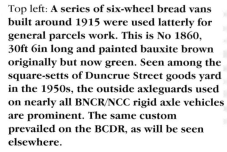

Left: The double horsebox of 1885 looked more substantial, though a timber underframe might have done with six wheels like those of 1890 built by the BCDR. Horseboxes were all numbered in the 200 series up to World War Two; what remained followed passenger brakes in the 400 series. No 257, seen here, and its fellows did not apparently survive the war. The device that allowed the top portion of the horses' door to rise when the lower half fell under its own weight is visible at the right-hand end.

Top right: **Eight carriage trucks were known to have been on the NCC's books, numbered 321-328. In this 1931 view, No 323 has been freshly done-up. The lettering may have been hand-painted, as LMS NCC is in the angular style used on NCC goods stock, quite unlike the parent company's practice.**

Centre right: **Breakdown vans used by most other companies were usually superannuated passenger stock, as we have seen, but York Road built some of these vehicles based on the 'brown van' design. No 3078, seen on 11th May 1967, has been refurbished by UTA, with new doors. Note the underframe: steel, with traditional 'outside' axleguards.**

Below: **The much-rebuilt BNCR saloon No 8 is seen in Belfast near the end of its life, painted in the faded remains of the GNR blue-and-cream livery that was bestowed on the Royal Train of 1953. Its last number was 152. When used as an Inspection saloon by the NCC, No 8 had an open observation platform at one end.** Derek Young.

Top left: **UTA No 162, seen at York Road on 29th February 1964, began life as NCC Dining car No 89. This ran as a trailer to the First class Dining/kitchen car No 88 from the 1924 Derby built batch.** Derek Young.

Centre left: **This was one of the coaches transferred from the mainland by the LMS in 1942 to make up for vehicles which had been destroyed in the German air raids on Belfast in 1941 which had caused great damage at York Road. No 196 (UTA No 387) was a suburban Third class, nine compartment carriage built at Derby in 1934. It is seen here, ex-works at York Road on 29th February 1964.** Derek Young.

Below: **York Road produced three 57ft Brakes, Nos 404-406, in 1936. The UTA renumbered them 613-615. This is No 613 on the traverser at the combined rail and road workshops built by the UTA at Duncrue Street and long since covered by the M2 motorway. The date is 16th July 1963.** Derek Young.

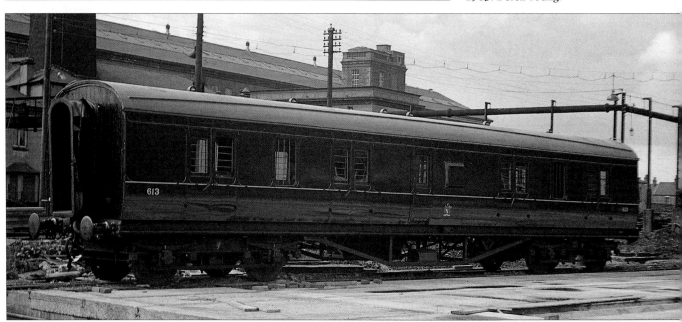

BELFAST & COUNTY DOWN RAILWAY

The first BCDR carriages came from Joseph Wright's then new establishment in Saltley in Birmingham, the order being for six First class and 12 Second class four-wheelers. There was no Third class and no significant increase in stock until the main line was extended to Downpatrick in 1858/59. Then the reconstituted Irish firm of Rogerson, Dawson and Russell supplied a quantity of both carriages and wagons including four First class six-wheelers. The remaining Composites and Seconds and the three horseboxes were all four-wheelers. Third class was created with the conversion of the old Wright Seconds. All that was needed was relabelling, no upholstery being involved. The Wright coaches lasted over-long with this impecunious company, several lingering into the 1880s.

The 'County Down' company had to endure 36 years of slow growth and indifferent management before its fortunes began to improve. It was still using rolling stock from its early years when engines and carriages to work the BHBR were ordered for the opening of the Bangor line in 1865. Eight Composites built by the Railway Carriage Co. of Oldbury were bought back for a trifling sum in 1867 when the junior company took over the working of its own line. Oldbury also provided stock for the Newcastle extension of 1869, including four Firsts, six Thirds, a Passenger brake and a horsebox. From the prices quoted, these may have been four-wheelers. These Thirds were the last pre-1886 stock to survive. They were six-wheelers when broken up in 1921. Only three further coaches were added in the 1870s, being six-wheel Thirds built with the utmost economy by the Metropolitan Carriage and Wagon Co. In 1884 the lost sheep of the BHBR were gathered into the BCDR fold. By then BCDR passenger stock had been numbered in one consecutive list. Nos 1-9 were Firsts, 10-24 Composites, 25-28 Seconds and 29-55 Thirds. Other coaching vehicles' remained in their individual lists until 1945. The main list became untidy when the 46 BHBR four-wheelers were renumbered 56-101. On that strange line coach numbering was a baffling nonsense.

Robert George Miller was BCDR Locomotive Superintendent from 1882 to 1919. Due to directors common to both railways, he was always in Bowman Malcolm's shadow and was frequently made to take the latter's advice on engine matters, despite having been trained by McConnell (of 'Bloomer' fame) on the LNWR Southern Division. Miller had come to Ireland as Loco Foreman of that LNWR satellite, the DNGR. On the BCDR he did well in a massive (for that line anyway) programme of carriage rebuilding that followed the BHBR take-over. In this field he does not seem to have suffered board interference, carriage policy being mainly a matter between Manager and Locomotive Superintendent. The new Manager was Joseph Tatlow, whose initial triumph was to persuade the Board to order 10 new six-wheelers from Oldbury. After that the pace quickened. The BCDR's own State Carriage came from Metropolitan in 1889, soon to be followed by ordinary coaches from both Metropolitan and Ashbury. The BCDR paid brief homage to the bogie coach in 1896/7 when Ashbury delivered 12. Six were Brake-thirds, the others Composites. They were 49ft 3in x 8ft 6in over body and rode on Fox's pressed steel bogies which had an 8ft wheelbase. In 1897 also, Ashbury built the celebrated Royal saloon, No 153, bow-ended with a clerestory roof and 43ft 6in by 8ft 6in over mouldings. No further carriages were ordered from outside for many years, Queen's Quay shops embarking on a building programme that continued until the early 1920s. Unfortunately there was insufficient room there for economical production of bogie stock and a competent team of coachbuilders were confined to turning out a variety of six-wheel designs. Three steam railcars, with engines by Kitson of Leeds and coach bodies from Metropolitan, came in 1905 and 1906. They were moderately successful but the power units had worn out by 1918. With plenty of life left in the cars themselves, they did provide the BCDR with a further three bogie vehicles for push-pull services. Hindsight is a great thing, but it is a pity that the still-prosperous company did not think of enlarging the two-road railmotor shed built for these cars to become the basis for a new coach-building facility that might have produced something better than the obsolescent six-wheelers still being presented to the travelling public in 1923.

Details of the 'standard' six-wheelers built by the BCDR in the twentieth century are given in the table below; the dates shown are those when the first of each type was made. A total of 109 carriages were built between 1903 and 1923, all had bodies 8ft 5in wide over mouldings.

A tradition of First class saloon accommodation on business train extended back to BHBR days, one of Miller's first tasks being to re-body five of these Saloons and give them an extra pair of wheels. Four of these Saloons had a Second class compartment at either end and the fifth had one Second and a Brake compartment. They were the last BHBR stock in use, being withdrawn around 1914. By then, there can have been little more than the original underframes left. One Saloon was grounded behind the wagon shop and the writer noticed BCDR-style panelling that seemed somehow odd, but it had been demolished before its significance was appreciated.

Traffic had increased in the brief boom after the First World War forcing the company to hire some six-wheelers from the GSWR, MGWR and GNR, for a while. The ancient Oldburys (Nos 33-38) forming a workmens' train were withdrawn in 1921, to be replaced by eight less ancient six-compartment Thirds from the GNR, class U3 of 1883/85. These lasted only to 1928, when the NCC supplied eight of Bowman Malcolm's similar Thirds, slightly younger than the U3s. Most were still going strong in 1943, their seats trimmed with American cloth and stuffed with horsehair. By then, wartime had put a strain on BCDR resources. The NCC was again turned to for help. With the LMS hav-

Class	Date	Body	Description/Seating 1st/2nd/3rd	Number built
First	1912	37ft 6in	5-compartment/40	4
First saloon	1916	35ft	divided into two sections/36	3
Brake-First/Second	1915	35ft	Van(7ft 3in) 2nd-1st-1st-2nd, 16/20/	2
Second	1905	37ft 6in	6-compartments/60	41
Brake-Second/Third	1905	35ft	Van(11ft 5in) 3rd-2nd-2nd-3rd, 20/20	2
Second/Third	1904	35ft	3rd-3rd-2nd-2nd-2nd-3rd 30/30	11
Third	1909	32ft 6in	six-compartment, 60	15
Third	1920	37ft 6in	seven-compartment, 70	14
Brake-Third	1903	35ft	Van(13ft 1in), four Third compartments, 40	17

ing replaced the coaches lost in the blitz, four ex-BNCR bogies were made available and refurbished at Dundalk works by the GNR. The coaches involved were two First-second and two eight-compartment Thirds which looked very smart in full BCDR livery when delivered to Queen's Quay where they were marshalled as one rake. Five of their predecessors were quickly snapped up for lineside use, two had already gone in a shunting mishap and the eighth, now on a GNR underframe, became the BCDR breakdown van. Owing to wartime shortages the 'new' bogie Thirds were supplied without dynamos for lighting and took their power supply via jumper cables from the ex-NCC Composites with which they were paired. While on the subject of carriage lighting it should be mentioned that the BCDR had adopted Pope's oil-gas illumination in 1893 and only the last 32 six-wheelers had Stone's electric lighting fitted when built. The Queen's Quay oil-gas plant was bombed in 1941. Fortunately the NCC had converted its own gaslit coaches by then and a replacement came from York Road.

By the 1930s the BCDR management was very conscious of the anachronistic appearance of its carriages in comparison with those of its neighbours and argued for a complete train of modern stock. They were given the funds for only two coaches which were built by R Y Pickering of Wishaw and delivered in 1938. They were the BCDR's first Tricomposites and it was as if no class of passenger was to be denied the unaccustomed pleasure of sampling the company's newest stock. With only one assistant, John L Crosthwait, who had succeeded Miller as Locomotive Engineer in 1920, had no drawing office to produce the working drawings for these carriages. These were

undertaken by the NCC draughtsmen at York Road, and that fount of information, J H Houston, has told us that Crosthwait considered a high-elliptical roof to be an unnecessary expense, so the new Tricomposites were given the low-elliptical roof profile used by the GNR in the 1890s. But they were none the worse for that. The remainder of the exterior design must also have been decided by the BCDR engineer, for there was moulded panelling of a new type that suited the 'Trios', numbered 120 and 121, very well. On underframes of standard LMS design with 9ft wheelbase bogies, these coaches ran splendidly and, from personal experience, I can say they were better than similar vehicles on the NCC. The compartments were laid out as follows; 3 Seconds, 2 Firsts, 2 Seconds and 2 Thirds.

BCDR coaching stock was renumbering in 1945, with gaps in the main carriage list being made good. Six-wheel Passenger brakes, which had been in their own list up to then, were integrated into the main list following the highest number on that, which was 183. They were now numbered 184-190. Vans Nos 5 and 9 retained their old numbers to replace gaps in the main list left by Second class carriage No 5, destroyed in the blitz, and Second-third Composite No 9, wrecked in the Ballymacarrett collision of 1945. Railmotors 1-3 filled other gaps becoming Nos 59, 72 and 173 respectively. Horseboxes 1-10 became 191-200. Bread vans (which had started life as fish vans and were branded thus throughout their BCDR careers) became 201-254. The two carriage trucks Nos 205 and 206, brought up the end of the list. All numbers from 1 to 206 were thus neatly occupied when BCDR stock was handed over to the UTA on 1st October 1948.

Finally, a brief mention of BCDR coach liv-

eries. Before Tatlow's arrival as Manager in 1885, carriages had been painted cheaply using teak stain costing one shilling a pound. The State Carriage was splendid in crimson lake when delivered in 1889 and its appearance was a handy weapon to use against the company's false economy. Crimson lake was adopted for all coaching stock from 1890 and that livery remained in use to the end. It was similar in hue to the crimson of LMS(NCC) carriages.

We do not know what nineteenth century coaching stock drawings may have perished when the Locomotive Engineer's office was burnt out during the Belfast blitz of 1941. Their loss was probably felt more by later historians than by the men on the shop floor for it seems that by this time the Queen's Quay coachbuilders had become so used to their standard styling that the last six-wheelers had been built without recourse to special drawings. It has been recounted that in the lunch break, the chargehand coachbuilder and his acolytes would gather in the Rising Tide bar at the corner of Scrabo Street to discuss the day's problems and that many of these would be solved on the bar counter with the aid of a finger dipped in beer!

Apart from the engine number, nothing has changed in this view of Queen's Quay terminus on 13th May 1950. The Bangor train behind No 208 was formed exclusively of six-wheelers. R C Riley

Right: Brake-third No 51, seen at Bangor on 30th June 1951, was one of the Oldbury six-wheelers delivered on Joseph Tatlow's instigation in 1888. They had straight sides and were 30ft by 8ft 6in over bodies. The Oldburys came out every summer for excursion work until withdrawn in September 1951.

Below: Tatlow also convinced the BCDR Board that they needed a proper State Carriage. The result was No 53, a six-wheeler built by Metropolitan Carriage & Wagon in 1889. It was 26ft by 8ft 6in over body with a central saloon and end compartments. It is seen at Queen's Quay sidings on 4th August 1949.

Right: The Ashbury bogie coaches were 9ft 3in by 8ft 6in. One of the Brake-thirds, No 143 shown here, awaits disposal after auction at Queen's Quay on 3rd July 1959. The very small Guard's compartment (8ft 1in) was enlarged by absorbing one of the original eight passenger compartments. These were only 5ft wide between partitions.

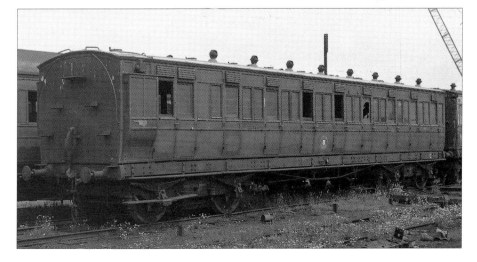

Top: **Royal Saloon 153 is in its final
condition at Bangor on 18th February
1950. Altered to what was called a
'working coach' in 1924, it was stripped of
its internal refinements and given a
second door on each side, to become the
Golfers Saloon on the Newcastle express
every Saturday until the closure of the
BCDR main line in January 1950. It was
found unsuitable for work on the Bangor
line, the only part of the BCDR to survive
the UTA's 1950 cull and was whisked away**
to the NCC shortly after I photographed it.
Thankfully, this historic carriage is still
around. Now in the hands of the
Downpatrick Steam Railway, the body is
scheduled for eventual restoration on a
replacement underframe.

Above: **Seen at Queen's Quay on 8th May
1950, Brake-third six-wheeler No 29 was
of the standard four-compartment design
of 1903. Some of these were built with**
partitions no higher than the seat-backs,
an arrangement seemingly designed to
encourage rowdy behaviour. Painted in
BCDR red before a UTA livery had been
decided on, the number 29 was applied to
the lookout, not standard practice on the
'County Down'.

Above and right: **The BCDR rail-motors were easily converted to push-pull working by removing the articulated power units, modifying their underframes and fitting a second carriage bogie. Being one class only, passengers were seated in a long saloon. The Ballymacarrett disaster of 1945 saw the end of auto-train working on both the BCDR and the GNR. Following their conversion, the very unusual twin headlights, lit by gas held in the reservoirs visible under the body, were retained. The clerestory was unglazed but ventilation was provided by means of horizontal codding, under the control of the Guard. This is car No 1, later 59 in the carriage list. It and No 2 (72) were 50ft by 8ft 6in over body and seated 60 passengers. The later and larger car No 3 (173) was 60ft 6in long and seated 76. These photographs were taken at Queen's Quay on 26th February 1951.**

Below: **When No 173 was outshopped after the 1945 accident as a Brake open Third, it was used on the Bangor business trains. In the first couple of days it was eagerly sought after by commuters, hungary for bogie stock. The snag was soon discovered, with only one door at each end, it took so long to unload its passengers that it soon reverted to the Holywood short workings**

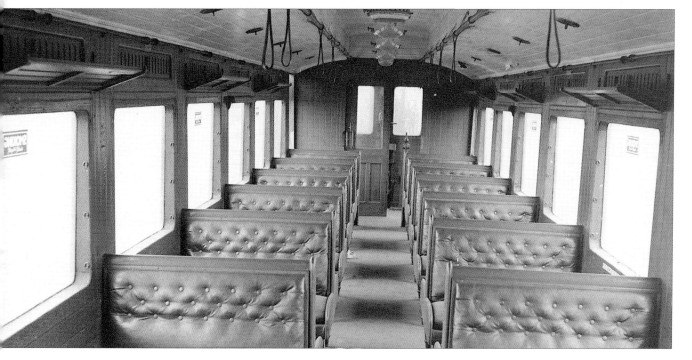

The coaches here are all 37ft 6in, the maximum length for six-wheelers on the BCDR. The most recent six-compartment Seconds were chosen for repainting in UTA green. Built between 1912 and 1921, they had been fitted with electric light. Some gaslit Seconds followed, such as No 68, (above) built in 1907, seen newly-repainted on 21st June 1950. The five-compartment Firsts of 1912, Nos 130-133 used exclusively on the Bangor line were gaslit and never repainted by UTA. No 130, (below) was photographed at Queen's Quay on 27th June 1950. The seven-compartment Thirds included the newest six-wheelers of all. No 167, (left) seen on the same date, was built in 1920 but the last came out as late as 1923.

Right: Saloons 2, 3 and 4 were built in 1916 as replacements of the last Belfast, Holywood & Bangor Railway coaches in service. Nos 2 and 4 were downgraded to Second class between the wars but were not popular and were kept for summer use when demand was at its peak. No 3 is seen at Queen's Quay on 18th July 1949.

Below: The Tricomposites Nos 120 and 121 were splendid vehicles. Their Third class accommodation was reasonable at 5ft 9in between partitions; Second class gave you 6ft and First class surpassed the Golfers' Saloon for cushioning while leg room was generous at 7ft 2½in. There were two Third, two First and five Second class compartments in its 57ft 1in by 9ft body. No 120 was photographed on 26th February 1951. The pair went to the NCC and were the only BCDR coaches to be numbered under the new UTA scheme.

Right: Two ex-BNCR bogie Thirds were purchased from the NCC with the two composites already referred to. Now BCDR 178, one of the pair is parked on 30th March 1950 in the wash siding for cattle wagons at Queen's Quay, though the cattle traffic has long since gone.

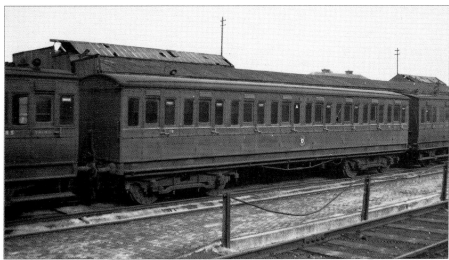

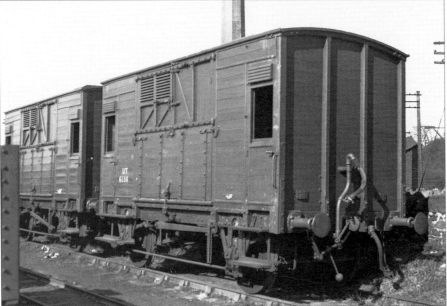

Above: **This six-wheel passenger Brake No 186, was built by Metropolitan Carriage & Wagon Company to the straight-sided outline of the previous Oldbury vans but with different mouldings. Queen's Quay works has given it a makeover in 1950, removing the skylight and glazing one of the luggage doors on each side to compensate. It was photographed on 23rd May 1950.**

Centre left: **The standard BCDR horsebox was stoutly made and after the UTA takeover found favour on the former NCC section in replacing the much older BNCR type. No 196 has been repainted at York Road and is seen at Larne Harbour on 10th March 1951 wrongly renumbered 6196. This was a number from the goods vehicle series.**

Bottom left: **Bread van No 203 lies idle in Queen's Quay yard on 1st April 1951. This was one of two vans originally built for the Ardglass fish traffic in 1917. These were a couple of inches taller than the previous two built in 1911, one of which can just be glimpsed to the right of the picture. With their rigid wheelbase of 17f I have often wondered whether they were ever allowed to work over the Ardglass Harbour tramway**

INDEPENDENTLY MINDED

In this chapter we will examine the carriages of two railways, the Sligo Leitrim & Northern Counties and the Dundalk, Newry & Greenore, which retained their independence and identity until closure, though in rather different circumstances. The SLNCR remained independent because it straddled the border and thus escaped the clutches of the GSR in 1925. The DN&G became part of the LMS at the British grouping in 1923 by dint of its LNWR parentage. However, it was isolated from the rest of the LMS lines in Ireland and was largely in a foreign country, in political terms anyway. It thus continued in its own way and though operated by the GNR from 1933 onwards, it remained, to all intents and purposes, an outpost of the LNWR, surviving its parent company by nearly 30 years.

The Dundalk, Newry & Greenore Railway

One of the later arrivals on the Irish railway map, the DNGR's coaching stock is undoubtedly the best documented of any company covered by this book. Astute diplomacy by the London & North Western Railway captured two rival companies, the Dundalk & Greenore and the Newry & Greenore, and reconstituted them as the DNGR in 1867. All the line's rolling stock, carriages, wagons and locomotives, were built at the LNWR's workshops at Wolverton, Earlestown and Crewe. Train services between Greenore and Dundalk began in May 1873 coinciding with the commencement of the LNWR steamship service between Holyhead and Greenore. The final part of the system, the line from Greenore to Newry did not open until August 1876.

Carriage-building for the DNGR had been planned well in advance. For the 1873 opening, three six-wheel Tricomposites and three four-wheel five-compartment Thirds were available, along with two four-wheel Passenger brakes. All numbered in one series from 1 to 8. Three horseboxes, Nos 17-19 came soon afterwards. The numerical gap was filled in 1876 with Nos 9 and 10, four-wheel Brakes, three first-second composites and another three four-wheel Thirds. The Trios were known as double composites on the LNWR and arranged Second-First-Luggage-First-Third. Nos 10-12 had two compartments for each class and were similar in length to Nos 1-3 at 30ft 6in. Width is stated to have been 8ft 3in, the standard LNWR dimension of the time, but may have been 8ft 6in for the Composites. The four-

wheel Brakes were 26ft by 7ft 4in, 8ft 1½in over lookouts. The 1876 Thirds were a throw-back to an earlier LNWR type,having four compartments. A further three horseboxes, Nos 20-22, were added in 1878. Few Irish lines could have matched this prodigality, for all the original stock had been disposed of by the early 1900s. Most of their replacements would last the life of the DNGR, and beyond. The new six-wheelers were solidly built, and smooth-riding as far as the Composites were concerned. The second numbers Nos 1 and 2, were built in 1909, with bodies 30ft by 8ft 6in arranged Second-Second-First-First-Coupe-First. The three bogie coaches, Nos 24-26 of 1899/1900, built for the through boat trains from Belfast owed more in their layout to GNR influence in that they had lavatories for all three classes and a Guard's compartment at one end. Their later careers have already been mentioned. Dimensions were 50ft by 8ft 6in though they were gas lit, doubtless much to GNR displeasure.

The new Thirds were an improvement, 30ft by 8ft 6in with five compartments and better leg-room, built between 1901 and 1909, they were numbered 3-6 and 14-16. The new generation of Passenger brakes were still inferior to their mainland contemporaries. The dimensions of these six-wheelers were 30ft 1in by 8ft 6in. Even the horseboxes were superseded by a batch of 1900/1 taking the old numbers. The last addition to the stock in 1906 was No 26, a covered carriage truck, which became, as we saw earlier, LMS NCC motor car van No 1806.

The writer's first sight of a DNGR train was in summer 1937, a completely unexpected apparition as we drew into Dundalk Junction on the GNR. It was beautifully turned out, including the engine in lined black livery and the gold-leaf carriage transfers sparkled in the sunshine. Only the DNGR crest might have been called a 'red cabbage' in place of the LNWR 'cauliflower', but was a pretty thing too, showing Britannia, complete with trident, shaking hands with Hibernia and her Irish wolfhound on a Celtic shore. In the background a GNR train steamed towards Greenore Harbour!

The Sligo, Leitrim & Northern Counties Railway

Was this railway the most Irish of them all? It suffered all the misfortunes endemic to the Irish lines and had few strokes of good luck. It relied heavily on local capital in a region with

few natural resources but blessed with railwaymen of the right calibre, it was a doughty fighter to the end.

The SLNCR's Act of Parliament had been obtained in 1875. Construction began at the Enniskillen end, allowing opening in stages until Carrignagat Junction, on the MGWR line 5¼ miles short of Sligo town, was reached in November 1882. The easterly flow of cattle traffic to the British markets was the line's mainstay throughout its 78 year existence. Its first rolling stock was purchased from the British Wagon Company by an SLNCR director and included two Composites, two Brake vans and a Third class carriage. Later coaching stock was from the Ashbury Company and included one horsebox and two carriage trucks. The straight-sided stock with raised mouldings, not unlike that supplied to the BCDR by Oldbury in the 1880s, became the hallmark of SLNCR passenger trains, though the typical formation in the Leitrim landscape was a long string of cattle wagons led by a handful of six-wheelers.

Carriage and wagon records appear to have been non-existent when R W Sparks came from the MGWR in 1919 as SLNCR Locomotive Engineer. Sparks wasted no time in remedying this deficiency, preparing working drawings for what would be a standard range of goods vehicles and making his own carriage and wagon diagram books. His records show an inheritance of 17 six-wheelers. These were; five six-compartment Thirds (Nos 12, 6, 8, 12, 13 and 14), six Brake-thirds (Nos 4, 5, 7, 15, 16, 18), four Tricomposites with two compartments for each class(Nos 9, 10, 11, 17) and two First-second composites with luggage-boots Nos 2 and 19, Wolverton-built cast-offs acquired from the DNGR in 1909.

A few more points about the six-wheelers may be of interest. There were at least two varieties of Brake-third. No 4 in its original form is shown on the diagram as having three compartments and an end van with both roof lookout and 'cabs'. It was 28ft 3in over body. No 15 had been photographed as approximating to a 'centre van' type, with one compartment at one end and two at the other. The surviving Trio, No 17, was renumbered 12 when the bogie stock came. The fate of the ex-DNGR coaches is uncertain. Perhaps two Composites from the GNR were intended as their replacements. One came in 1929. SLNCR No 2 had been GNR No 84, class R5 of 1885, arranged Second-First-First-Second. No 3 arrived some six years later. Formerly GNR 95, class R6 of 1888, it was different in having a double-door locker in the middle. One remembers it as the solitary coach on a cattle special. The cushions were moth-eaten but tolerable; this was in 1948. By that time the day-to-day passenger business was in the hands of the railbuses and the state-of-the-art Walker railcar that modest wartime profits had rendered affordable.

As soon as Sparks had settled down at Manorhamilton to put the stock in good order, the luckless SLNCR became a target for the Civil War insurgents and much of his work was undone. He had begun to modernise the Ashbury carriages by converting the Thirds to a 'bus-type' layout with wide windows and turn-over seats. No 12 was altered in this way, with a smaller section for non-smokers, as was Brake-third No 4. The latter would survive to the end, but No 12 was destroyed with at least three others, Tricomposites Nos 9, 10 and 11. Those numbers will be familiar to the fortunate few who recall the SLNCR, for they were given to the bogie coaches, paid for by the state, which replaced those destroyed. These also were Tricomposites. No 9 was a Brake-tricomposite arranged; Brake, Third, Third, First, Third, Second, Coupé (half-Second) with end lights. Incidentally, Sparks' diagram refers to the van being 10ft 3½in wide over 'cab' mould-

ings. The width of all three was otherwise 9ft 1½in over mouldings and the body length was 44ft 6in. Bogie centres were 29ft 9in apart, the bogie wheelbase being 7ft 6in. The layout of Nos 10 and 11 was: Third. Third. First, an open Third section seating 32 with two doors on each side, Second and Coupé Second. The partitioning of the solitary First class into smoking and non-smoking sections has frequently been remarked upon. Nos 9 and 11 had electric light, No 10 did not, being a 'daytime' coach, though all three were steam-heated. The trio have been criticised for their short body length and anachronistic appearance. The last SLNCR engineer, G F Egan, was more concerned at having to keep them on their home ground, for it was soon found that the bearings were inadequate and the axleboxes ran hot at any speeds higher than the moderate ones achieved on their own line.

It has often been wondered why the builders, Hurst Nelson and Company of Motherwell, should have been instructed in the year 1924 to provide clerestory roofs for these vehicles. It appears to have been entirely due to the dedication of R W Sparks to his job. He was prepared to perpetuate the external appearance of the Ashbury bodywork but to add a clerestory was to make a statement that here were three vehicles superior to anything the

company had owned before. Sparks was an accomplished draughtsman. I have often imagined him alone in his corrugated-iron office - perhaps on a dark night with Manorhamilton yard silent below, producing among his many other designs a complete set of working drawings, so complete that Hurst Nelson's draughtsman had only to make tracings before handing them to the shop foreman. When it came to the clerestory, his former colleagues at the Broadstone sent a blueprint of what had been done for the Saloons built in Cusack's time on the MGWR.

Sparks introduced one further class of coaching vehicle, a seven-ton parcels and fish van. Four of these four-wheelers were built at Manorhamilton, numbered 3, 4, 5 and 7 in a separate series which hints at earlier vans of that kind. The new ones were 15ft 2in by 8ft on a 9ft 6in wheelbase. Piped for the vacuum brake, their double-sheeted bodies were painted passenger maroon with yellow lettering. They saw little use in later days. By 1925 G F Egan had taken over at Manorhamilton and nothing further has so far been found about his remarkable predecessor. Alas for the intricate glazing of those clerestories, by the 1940s they had been canvassed over as had those of the neighbouring GNR.

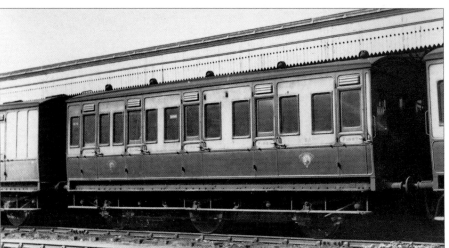

Above: **All three of the last Greenore carriage types are illustrated in this view of DNGR No 1 *Macrory* (named after the company's solicitor) and train on the Newry section in 1933. It shows, from left a five-compartment Third, a First-second with a Coupé and the standard passenger Brake van.**

Left: **A closer look at the Composite No 1, arranged Second, Second, First, First, Coupé First, seen in the Greenore bay platform at Dundalk Junction on 14th April 1948. No 1 was later preserved and is now part of the collection of the Ulster Folk & Transport Museum. H C Casserley.**

Top right: **Third class six-wheeler No 16 was one of the DNGR coaches transferred to the NCC by the parent company in 1933 following cut-backs after the disastrous strike of that year.**

Right: **This four-wheel Third was originally DNGR No 4, built at Wolverton in 1872. Sold to the CBSCR in 1901, it is seen at Inchicore in early GSR days, repainted in the purple-lake livery, fully lined-out and numbered 7B.** H Richards collection.

Centre right: **The Bandon was glad to have Greenore cast-offs, Wolverton built them to last. Luggage-composite No 61B had been one of three built in 1872. In this view dated May 1946, the coach is in GSR crimson livery, lined in yellow.** H Richards collection.

Bottom right: **Ashbury Third class six-wheeler, SLNCR No 8, was in good order when photographed in 1933. One oil lamp serves two compartments and this company's method of hanging carriage doors on the right shows up well in this view. We are told that there was no firm rule on which way doors should be hung in earlier days and it is of little consequence on today's railways. Look closely for another mild eccentricity. Six-wheelers on the SLNCR were braked on one pair of end wheels and on the middle pair.**

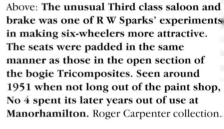

Above: **The unusual Third class saloon and brake was one of R W Sparks' experiments in making six-wheelers more attractive. The seats were padded in the same manner as those in the open section of the bogie Tricomposites. Seen around 1951 when not long out of the paint shop, No 4 spent its later years out of use at Manorhamilton.** Roger Carpenter collection.

Centre left: **The bogie Brake-composite No 9 had been repainted not long before the SLNCR closed, but Mr Egan was apologetic that he had only a wagon painter at Manorhamilton and the work had obviously not come up to his professional expectations. 'SECOND' transfers now replaced 'THIRD' on the carriage doors. The scene is the SLNCR bay platform at Enniskillen on 15th August 1957.**

Bottom left: **Tricomposite No 10 was well known as the 'daytime' coach as it never had artificial light. This 1933 view was fortunately secured before the clerestory was canvassed over and its fenestration can be admired. The one First class compartment was divided on the long axis to make smoking and no smoking sections.**

Top right: **The electric light switch on the end of this Tricomposite tells us that it must be No 11, dozing in the evening sunshine at Enniskillen on 15th August 1957.**

Centre right: **In 1925, the SLNCR's Ashbury horsebox was wrecked in a shunting mishap on Sligo Quay. The GSR accepted liability and presented the Sligo company with a replacement, an ex-WLWR horsebox No 1027 of 1870, thus making sure that the SLNCR was not given anything newer than the original. The second No 1 is at Manorhamilton, its livery was dark green with yellow lettering. The date is 25th April 1959, the line has closed, the auction has taken place and Manorhamilton will soon be without a railway.**

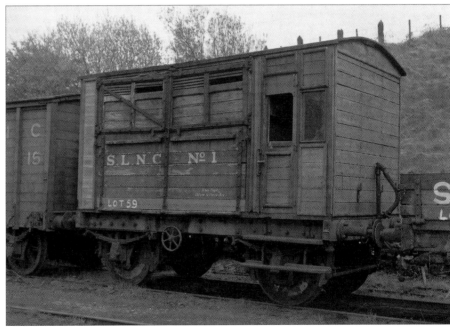

Below and below right: **Side and end elevations of R W Sparks' neat little parcels No 5, in the remains of its maroon livery with yellow lettering, seen at Collooney on 19th May 1959.**

FROM THE UTA TO THE PRESENT

The conventional railway carriage does not figure largely in the railway policy of the UTA. From its very beginning, what railways that would be retained were to be operated by diesel railcars; freight would be road-based, thus diesel-electric locomotives would be unnecessary. The new regime was starting with a blank sheet of paper and it was fortunate that engineering and operating staff of the right calibre were at hand in the old NCC's York Road headquarters. We have seen that, in 1948, the NCC was in limbo between its old masters and the UTA, but management was busy behind the scenes. The war-ravaged York Road workshops were in no condition to begin rolling-stock manufacture, but railway land was available for new road/rail workshops near the NCC's Belfast terminal at Duncrue Street The works were in production by the early 1950s but the UTA's first new railway carriage was Dining car No 87, completed in 1950 at the Dunmurry shops of the former Northern Ireland Road Transport Board situated between Belfast and Lisburn. As you may guess, there was no rail access but some 'brown vans' and a new design of goods brake van were produced here. There is an interesting view of No 87 on a low loader being manoeuvred around Donegall Square in Belfast in Mark Kennedy's book *The LMS In Ireland* (Midland Publishing, 2000)

In 1948, the NCC had acquired eight quite presentable bogie carriages from BR's London Midland Region. Appropriately, they had been Derby-built by the Midland Railway, dating from 1908-10. The manner of their acquisition was rather strange. A local railway enthusiast (not the author), in conversation with one of York Road's top brass, mentioned the GNR's recent purchase of several redundant LMS carriages. The reaction was something like, 'What! We must have some too'. The coaches had arrived by the end of the year and were given the numbers 20-27 in the NCC list. Only one is recorded as entering service in 1948. This was No 22, a seven-compartment suburban First, 50ft by 9ft. It may be regarded as the last NCC coach of all, as the remainder were outshopped in under the UTA regime in 1949 and 1950. Sent to the Bangor line in 1949, No 22 was still in LMS red but saw little use even though re-branded Second class where it stood in the Queen's Quay sidings before returning to the NCC where it became a First-second composite. A similar vehicle, No 23, began its new career as a Composite. The remaining ex-Midland coaches were two Brake-thirds both with six compartments, one 48ft and the other 50ft, and four eight-compartment Thirds, one pair being 48ft and the other two 50ft.

For the new rolling stock, LMS standard 60ft underframes and bogies were ordered in quantity from BR. Something like 45 sets were obtained mostly for the railcars then on the drawing board. Duncrue Street surprised us by building two suburban bogies for the Bangor line. No 351 was a Brake-second with seven compartments (84 seats) and No 361, a First-second having four compartments for each class seating 32 and 48 respectively. Both were snatched back to the NCC very quickly. A quantity of corridor stock was built in time for the 'Festival Express' of 1951. There were six side-corridor Thirds with seven compartments and two lavatories, six open Thirds divided in three sections accommodating 16, 24 and 16 with end lavatories. Two Brake-third side corridors had six compartments and one lavatory while two side-corridor Composites displayed some ambivalence. One was First-second, the other was First-third. The former had three First and four Second, the latter had four Thirds. Each had lavatories at both ends. These 18 carriages were originally numbered in an extended NCC series commencing at 301 with several gaps which may have been left for further construction.

It had been mid-1949 before the Authority decided on rolling stock liveries. UTA bus colours followed NIRTB practice. The upper panels used a shade of eau-de-nil that reminded one of a concoction called Aungier's Emulsion forcibly fed to the young of my generation; this was much lighter than, say, the colour applied to railbuses of the SLNCR that was closer to the usual 'Nile' green. However, an ex-BNCR bogie Third was experimentally painted in bus colours, though without the dark green waistband. With upper mouldings picked out in green, the effect was quite good. But like the 'two-tone' paintwork of 1950s motor cars, this cost more, and the boring all-over Brunswick green was adopted for UTA coaches, with yellow lining along the waist and yellow class numerals for First and Second only. Coach numerals used small bus-type transfers at first. Later, a horribly bilious light green was given to some suburban coaches, but did not last long. The UTA roundel, with the obligatory red hand in a shield, began to be applied in 1951. Once the green livery had been decided upon, intensive repainting took place. At Queen's Quay, a second paint shop (the old BCDR railmotor shed) was opened and much NCC rolling stock was dealt with there. As for BCDR carriages, only bogie stock and the later six-wheelers were repainted, along with two Passenger brakes, horseboxes and bread vans. Most of what was left were marked with red crosses of condemnation, reminding us of what we had learnt of London in the Great Plague. Apart from very old (1880s) stock scrapped in 1951, the rest were retained until the BCDR Abandonment Order had been obtained in 1953 and wholesale auctioning of surplus stock began. Before that, the GNR had been desperately short of coaches for summer excursions and borrowed several antiques for a few summers. The rate at which their paintwork deteriorated was a measure of how well they had previously been looked after by the hard-up BCDR. As the Bangor line was progressively equipped with multi-engined diesel sets (MEDs), the NCC section was glad enough to take the remaining BCDR carriages. Only then did any renumbering of the latter take place. Numbers that clashed with those in the NCC list had 1000 added.

Meanwhile, the ranks of good-quality NCC coaching stock were being steadily depleted as the dieselisation programme continued. Carriages entered Duncrue Street to emerge as railcars, driving trailers or intermediate cars, everything between the high-elliptical roofs and the old underframes being replaced. After the 1958 share-out of GNR stock, the acquisition of a variety of randomly numbered coaches obliged the UTA to adopt a renumbering scheme. Harold Houston was given this job; his solution was unconventional in that it was based on odd numbers for non-corridor stock and evens for corridor. Powered vehicles had always followed the original NCC 1-4 series but by 1967 this had extended into the 70s. A further series had to be found for the GNR railcars. Intermediate trailers are in the 500 series from the beginning. What may be called 'steam stock' were given block numbers as follows; Saloons 150-159, Catering vehicles 160-179, Firsts 180-189, Brake-firsts 190-199, Brake-composites 200-269, Composites 270-299, First-seconds 300-449 and Brake-seconds 450-499. Other coaching vehicles were numbered in the sequence 600-699. The redeeming feature of this scheme bore the Houston touch. No doubt as a clue for baffled enthusiasts like the author, all renumbered coaches carried a painted 'X' followed by the old number, at the right hand end of the solebar.

It has not been my intention to attempt a complete outline of Irish carriage liveries, but one notes that the Brunswick green era on the UTA lasted little more than 10 years. The change came with a curious attempt at 'regionalisation', curious because the system by this time had been pared down to the bone. The NCC, GNR and BCDR lines were commemorated in 'regional' liveries, LMS red and white was applied to stock on the NCC, blue and white for GNR (but lighter blue than before) and a shade of olive green faintly echoing the old BCDR loco green, again with white, for the handful of MEDs needed to work the 12 miles to Bangor. The 'white', at least on the ex-NCC lines, was in fact a very pale grey. But more rapid changes were at hand. The UTA was imploding and another Act of Parliament sundered road and rail (for good, we thought) and set up Northern Ireland Railways. In the transitional period, 1966, the UTA's first diesel-electric railcar sets - the 70 class - were introduced. The unpowered intermediate coaches built to run in these sets which were built at York Road are worthy of mention as representing the last flowering of railway coachbuilding in Belfast. Handsomely turned out in the new maroon and white livery, and attractively trimmed with deep blue upholstery in the First class and red in the Second. They were side-corridor coaches, six were second class with seven compartments, three were Brake-ended with four compartments. One was all-First, another a Composite with two compartments each and the third all Second class. All had two lavatories. Apart from carrying the cables for multiple-unit operation, there was nothing to distinguish them from loco-hauled stock. Two driving-trailers were also built in the same style with gangways at both ends. These coaches were numbered 701-726. They utilised the 57ft underframes of the NCC J11 ten-compartment suburban Thirds. This class was a mixture of stock built at Derby and Wolverton between 1925 and 1939, which

was transferred to the NCC during the wars. The coaches were equipped with new bogies fitted with SKF roller bearings.

After this the story in Northern Ireland is dominated by BR Mark 2 coaches. The 80 class railcars introduced between 1974 and 1978 were built by BREL at Derby using adapted Mark 2 bodyshells. They were used on the three former NCC routes and the Bangor to Portadown service, the latter brought about by the reopening of the Belfast Central line. A little earlier in 1970, locomotive-hauled trains once agin took over NIR's share of the cross-border 'Enterprise' services. Three Hunslet diesel-electric locomotives were acquired fitted for push-pull working with a loco at either end for an eight-coach rake or one locomotive hauling a shortened set, with a driving-trailer at the other end. Eight modified Mk 2Bs were bought. These were an open First, four open Seconds, one Catering car with propane gas cooking and two Second class driving/brake trailers. Double glazing, pressure ventilation, electric heating, fluorescent lighting and

public address facilities were fitted. The open First came complete, the other seven coaches came as bodyshells and were fitted out in Belfast. The new 'Enterprise' saw passenger numbers begin to climb. Two years later in 1972 five more Mark 2C coaches, a First-class driving trailer and four open Seconds, arrived. Another 12 Mk2B were bought from BR in 1980. These were ten Firsts and two Brake-firsts. The latter were converted to Brake-standard generator vans and the Firsts were reclassified to Standard class. In 1982 further acquisitions included a Mk2F Dining car and allowed a second 'Enterprise' set to be formed to augment the weekday services. From the early 1980s the Belfast-Dublin expresses made up of the Mark 2s, were handled by General Motors diesels until the de Dietrich stock was introduced in 1997. In 2004 new Spanish built railcars will take over local services in Northern Ireland and this brings the history of the railway carriage in the north of Ireland to a full stop, as far as this book is concerned anyway.

Above right: W class 2-6-0 No 101 _Lord Massereene_ is at the head of eight brand-new coaches forming 'The Festival Express' introduced in 1951. The train, seen here on 20th June of that year, left Londonderry at 8.30am each weekday and worked back from Belfast at 5.25pm. The formation includes a three coach portion for Portrush consisting of a Brake-third, side-corridor Third and First-third. The five coaches for Derry were a side-corridor Third, open Third, Dining car, First-second composite and Brake-third.

Right: Bain suburban First No 22, which came from the English Midland Railway, forms part of a Holywood service on 9th May 1949. It retained the LMS lake livery during its short time on the BCDR section.

Top left: **Another of the Bain coaches, eight-compartment No 24, is seen in UTA green livery at York Road in the 1950s.**

Below: **The apparently new coaches that appeared at York Road in 1966/67 are discussed in the text. They were intermediates for the new DEMUs. This is No 725, a side-corridor Second in the new maroon and white livery.** Derek Young.

Bottom: **Both Northern Ireland Railways and CIE turned to BR for their coaching stock in the 1970s. A number of Mark 2 coaches were bought when the 'Enterprise Express' reverted to loco-haulage at the start of that decade. One of these carriages, No 930, seen here at Inchicore works, was the former BR Mark 2C No 5573.** Des Mc Glynn

Below: As mentioned earlier, the last carriages built to the Irish loading gauge were those constructed by Cravens from 1963 onwards. The last batch of these was actually built at Inchicore from parts supplied by the UK firm. Craven buffet car

No 1508 is seen here at Dromod next to ex-BR Mark 1 BSK No 34566, now CIE No 3184, converted to a Heating van at Derby in 1972. The difference in the width of the two vehicles is most noticeable.

Bottom: CIE also acquired Mark 2 stock from British Rail Engineering in the 1970s. A rake of these is seen at Heuston station in Dublin (the former Kingsbridge) in the 1980s. Both, Donal Murray

EPILOGUE

Since completing this review, I came across a critique, written over a century ago in an issue of the *Locomotive Magazine*, levelled at carriage designers. Too much attention had been given to external appearance, the extravagance of delicately moulded cornices and paneling took precedence over passenger comfort and internal finishes. Implicit in this was realisation that the railway carriage was built to last too long, an undoubted fact that took some time to penetrate railway management. It was a two-edged sword, Irish railways generally being forced as we have seen to retain and maintain obsolescent rigid-wheelbase carriages for economy's sake even though patronage was being lost to road vehicles whose relative convenience helped to overcome a lack of comfort that persisted until after the Second World War and was remedied as much by highway engineering as by improvement in vehicle design.

The Milne Report of 1948 made unfavourable comparison of the high average age of CIE rolling stock to that of its neighbour the GNR. The latter had from its inception progressively eliminated all the vehicles it had inherited. The writer's partiality for the GNR may have obscured its shortcomings. To wait until 1951 before abolishing Second class was surely a mistake. The K15 open Thirds of 1935 were commendable only for their two by two seating, and the small quantity of Bredin side-corridor Thirds produced by the indigent GSR equalled the standards being set at that time by the LMSR in Britain and trickling into Ulster by way of the NCC. In the writer's opinion, the degree Third class comfort achieved under W A Stanier on the LMS was eclipsed only by Hawksworth on the post-war Great Western. Then came the BR Mark 1s, whose side-corridor versions continued the LMS tradition, but once the travelling public was dragooned into liking the open Third I dare to suggest we were back to the K15, with an extra toilet. Unfortunately the high cost of producing a seven or eight compartment coach with sliding doors to the corridor and square yards of African hardwood veneers (all different) ensures that we shall never see its like again outside a Heritage railway, as they are now called. Not so long ago, 'airline comfort' had replaced 'Pullman comfort' as a catch-phrase. Now we have Economy class and it may be that the limitations of the British loading gauge being imposed on Irish rolling stock will force designers into adopting airline standards of discomfort. Deep vein thrombosis on rails?

Below: **Built by BREL at Derby in the mid 1980s to the BR Mk 3 design, the final fitting out of these carriages was done at Inchicore works. Standard No 7136 carries the Iarnród Éireann decals when seen in the carriage sidings at Heuston station.**

Bottom: **The last new locomotive hauled, or in this instance pushed, carriages supplied to run in Ireland, are those built by de Dietrich in France in the late 1990s for CIE and NIR for use on Belfast to Dublin services.** Both photos, courtesy CIE